new Tapas

TODAY'S BEST BAR FOOD FROM SPAIN

Santa María # 65

- Chips de yuca
- Anchoas con pan con tomate
- Mojama de atún con cebolla tierna y aceite de oliva
- Cecina de león
- Ensalada de castañas y calabaza y queso feta
- "Rovellons" con apio y mantequilla de cacahuete en ensalada
- Empanadillas de setas y pato confitado
- Ancas de rana marinadas con salvia y gengibre
- Guiso de caracoles con tortilla japonesa
- Sushi de verduras con salvia
- Maki de aguacate y pepino
- Maki de gamba y lechón rebozado
- Sushi variado
- Huevos de codorniz escalfados con pisto y chistorra
- "Rovellons botó" a la plancha
- Alcachofas guisadas con berengenas
- Tantan de vedellona
- Salteado de arroz integral con shitake, espárragos y judías
- Truchas de río con acelga, champiñones y cecina
- Bacalao con bom-ató y encurtidos
- "Civet de jabalí con manzana
- Canelleras de vedellona, col lombarda y patata
- Hígado de pato con pera y pimienta sichuan
- Suntido de quesos

* A partir de 3 comensales
sólo se sirve menu degustación *

≡ Postres ≡

- Piña colada con chupa-chups
- Helado de caki, plumb-cake y toffe
- Manzana reineta con bizcocho de frutos secos y helado de chocolate
- Trufas de chocolate

FIONA DUNLOP

new Tapas

TODAY'S BEST BAR FOOD FROM SPAIN

THUNDER BAY
P·R·E·S·S

San Diego, California

PHOTOGRAPHY BY JAN BALDWIN

To the fast-developing taste-buds of Oskar and Archie

THE BASQUE REGION 9

CATALONIA 33

RIOJA and OLD CASTILE 65

Thunder Bay Press
An imprint of the Advantage Publishers Group
5880 Oberlin Drive, San Diego, CA 92121-4794
www.thunderbaybooks.com

Copyright © Octopus Publishing Group Ltd 2002
Text copright (with the exception of the recipes) © Fiona Dunlop 2002

All notations of errors or omissions should be addressed to Thunder Bay Press, Editorial Department, at the above address. All other correspondence (author inquiries and permissions) concerning the content of this book should be addressed to Mitchell Beazley, an imprint of Octopus Publishing Group Limited, 2-4 Heron Quays, London E14 4JP, England.

ISBN-13: 978-1-57145-861-2
ISBN-10: 1-57145-861-1

Library of Congress Cataloging-in-Publication Data
Dunlop, Fiona, 1952-
    New tapas : today's best bar food from Spain / Fiona Dunlop.
        p. cm.
    ISBN 1-57145-861-1
    1. Appetizers. 2. Cookery-Spain I. Title.

    TX740   .D863 2002
    641.8'12'0946--dc21

                                    2002071266

Printed in China.

2 3 4 5 6 09 08 07 06 05

CONTENTS

INTRODUCTION

In the last decade or so, tapas have conquered the world, radiating from their Hispanic source to tease the taste buds of anyone in search of a generous snack to accompany a glass of wine. Yet such pan-national culinary clones are mere shadows of the real thing, found only in Spain. Racy flavors, high contrasts, generous doses of virgin olive oil, ultrafresh ingredients, fearless use of offal, and obsessive use of salt cod or cured ham—these are just some of the hallmarks of Spanish tapas. Such a gastronomic dance does not seem far removed from the emotional highs, lows, and syncopated rhythms of flamenco, an iconic representation of Spain itself.

Naturally enough, much tipsy speculation has taken place over the origins of tapas. Linguistically, the meaning is a plural extension of the word *tapa* ("lid"), from *tapar* ("to cover"), allegedly referring to slices of cheese or ham used to cover glasses of sherry in the hot, insect-infested bars of Andalucía. From these prosaic beginnings, so the story goes, came the tradition of serving small portions of bar food free with a glass of beer, wine, or sherry. An alternative theory originates from the thirteenth century, when the Castilian king, Alfonso X, surrendering to doctor's orders to recuperate from an illness, spent long days in bed, sipping small glasses of restorative wine accompanied by reduced portions of food. His recovery was so painless that a royal decree was announced, ordering taverns to serve wine only if accompanied by a snack.

Yet another, more down-to-earth theory equates tapas with the routines of the rural working day, tiding over appetites and boosting energy in a climate not always conducive to huge meals or hard labor. Pre- or postsiesta, grazing was the way to go for Spain's agricultural masses.

Whatever their starting point, tapas have moved on and are now inextricably linked to the Spanish way of life. They have generated the *tapeo* (tapas bar-hopping): a unique, mobile institution that brings swarms of families out onto the streets when the heat of the day has passed, to stroll, gossip, and stop for a drink—and, naturally, a tapa or two. The continuation of the habit is ensured by the presence of many generations, from grandpas to babies, while floors scattered with used paper napkins, cigarette butts, olive pits, mussel shells, and the odd errant anchovy all point clearly to the lip-smacking gusto of the activity.

There is no sitting around at isolated tables at an appointed hour, a victim to the whims of restaurant staff. The tapeo is something else: seemingly spontaneous, convivial, and informal, it occurs within customary time slots on a year-round basis. Ever different, the Basques opt for the word *poteo*, a derivative of *potes* ("pots" or "jars"), from which wine or cider was once drunk.

Traditionally, each bar cooked up only one tapas specialty, and this enforced peripatetic snacking on a population only too happy to prolong its voluble socializing. Drunkenness is rare; while spirits and decibels soar, excess alcohol is rapidly absorbed by sporadic feeding. You still find unique house specialties in smaller towns, but today's bars are more likely to chalk up a list of tapas and *raciónes* ("rations," or larger portions) of the day, providing bar stools so that aficionados can eat in comfort using a knife and fork—those little "lids," after all, are getting bigger and bigger. Again, the exception comes from the Basque region, where tapas are replaced by *pintxos* (or *pinchos*), finger snacks that resemble French canapés and scale new heights of diversity and elaborateness.

All this is part of the post-Franco folkloric revival" (a term coined by anthropologist T. Seppilli in 1992) is galloping ahead, highlighting local delicacies (anything from blood sausage, legumes, or organic cured ham to a snail or a quail) that may even be produced in a specific valley or village. This is nurturing a taste for quality. One exception is the ubiquitous *ensaladilla* ("little salad" or Russian salad), a tapa of canned vegetables smothered in mayonnaise that just won't go away. For

"Floors scattered with used paper napkins, cigarette butts, olive pits, mussel shells, and the odd errant anchovy all point clearly to the lip-smacking gusto of the activity. There is no sitting around at isolated tables at an appointed hour, victim to the whims of restaurant staff during the long wait for the chef's creations."

groundswell, an awakening to the sophisticated *nueva cocina* (new cuisine) that is galvanizing chefs into producing ever-more-inventive juxtapositions of ingredients and flavors. The initial impetus came from France via the Basques, and has since conquered local cuisine from Seville to Barcelona, Madrid to Salamanca. This renaissance has inspired most of the recipes in this book, which were created by young chefs in search of exciting gastronomic departures. There remain, too, the tapas classics, whose earthy flavors are unbeatable reflections of Spanish history, landscapes, and produce, and which differ radically from region to region.

Few tapas are universal in Spain; local produce is paramount. The "rural-

foreigners bemused by its similarity to 1960s airline food, the ensaladilla does raise questions as to the gastronomic discernment of this tapas-consuming nation. But then the French still snack on *croque monsieur*, so why not? There has to be some sort of atavistic yearning at work here. Mayonnaise itself appears again and again, whether straight out of a jar or as garlic-enhanced *aioli*.

The gastronomic euphoria of the last two decades goes hand in hand with Spain's newfound prosperity and awareness of the outside world. These, in turn, have led Spaniards to a greater pride in their own roots and cultural identity. Regionalism is king and *Denominación de Origen Controllado*, or DOC, labels of regulated quality, are proliferating; once used only for the country's wines as *Denominación de Origen* (DO) or with the attached *Calificada (DOCa)* for Rioja, this type of quality control now extends to foodstuffs such as white beans or suckling pigs.

Today's well-traveled chefs are concocting fusion food that in some cases reflects Spain's complex and cosmopolitan history. The wheel turns full circle to reintegrate Arab contrasts of flavors originally brought to the country by the Moors. In the same way, there is a revival of the Roman art of fish preserving. The basis of Spanish cuisine continues to be dominated by New World products: the potato, tomato, fava bean, and chili pepper. Add Phoenician, Greek, and Jewish input and you come to realize that by tasting Spanish tapas, you are tasting a good part of the globe, yet the cuisine was developed long before the term "fusion food" was coined.

In selecting tapas bars for this book, I have concentrated on places where the chefs serve evolved recipes that use relatively universal ingredients. It is the tapas capitals, such as Madrid, Seville, and San Sebastián, that are forging ahead in terms of creativity. Following closely behind are the traditionally less tapas-oriented cities of Barcelona and Valencia, bringing an extra kick of Catalan designer know-how in the case of the former, and cosmopolitan influences in the latter. In contrast, rural tapas bars are generally atmospheric relics of traditional tapas bars, left far behind in the tapeo rivalry of the cities.

So who exactly are these new tapas masters? Some of the best new tapas are coming out of bars that are combined with restaurants. Most chefs remain faithful to their native regions despite the experience of working in Madrid. Some have trained professionally and

worked with luminaries of the restaurant world; some are self-taught enthusiasts who have climbed the kitchen ladder. "Grandma's example" is often part of the equation, too, helping ensure the survival of time-honored culinary methods.

The bottom line is always one of respect for the innate qualities of the ingredients, a passion for the art, and a truly genuine desire to satisfy the customers. Celebrity tapas chefs are few and far between (Catalonia and the Basque region being two exceptions, as their marketing prowess comes hand-in-hand with economic acumen), due partly to that *mañana* cliché: live for today, since who knows what tomorrow will bring?

As Spanish cuisine evolves, so the rest of the world is beginning to see Hispanic produce exported along with vastly improved wines; chorizo, *jamón serrano* (literally "sawn ham," but cured like all *jamón*), virgin olive oil, sherry vinegar, *bacalao* (salt cod), and *boquerónes* (pickled anchovies) can all be found worldwide. In the other direction, the Spaniards have adopted smoked salmon, pâté, caviar, Roquefort, and cream cheese and even, in a handful of cases, started looking at Japanese sushi for tapas inspiration.

We love Spain because it is a world apart, but globalization continues to march on. The best we can do is keep in step, follow new Hispanic trends without forgetting the best of the old, practice the tapeo in Spain itself, and, above all, bring tapas into our homes. More than gastronomic indulgence, some of these dishes represent examples of the famous Mediterranean diet and embody that essentially Spanish attitude to life: enjoyment of the present. So go for it! The tapas will disappear in a flash—and after all, tomorrow never comes.

THE BASQUE COUNTRY

María Agustina Ostiz
Baserri

Iñaki Gulin
Álex Montiel
La Cuchara de San Telmo

Josecho Marañón
Mari Carmen Marañón
Manuel Marañón
Bar Txepetxa

Patxi Bergara
Blanca Ameztoy
Bar Bergara

*T*he road known as "the mountain highway" swings and dips from Navarra through the rugged Pyrenees before it finally descends into the Bay of Biscay. It runs through a landscape of craggy peaks, pine forests, *caserios* (stone farmhouses with steeply pitched roofs), Alpine-style chalets, verdant meadows, and the odd herd of cows and flock of sheep; that is, if you can see this at all. The Basque climate is characterized by *sirimiri*, a persistent drizzle that envelops the landscape.

The road leads to Europe's highest density of tapas bars. Your destination: San Sebastián, a grandiose nineteenth-

mere hop over the Pyrenees, an area that helped accelerate the influence of Gallic *nouvelle cuisine*. Spanish *nueva cocina* kicked off in the Basque country in the late 1970s, further stimulated by the region's gastronomic *txokos*, or brotherhoods, that have focused local epicures over the last century.

The Basque region claims the world's highest number of gourmet restaurants per capita. With the evolution of alternative txokos devoted to a single product—potatoes from Álava, black kidney beans from Tolosa, salmon from the Bidasoa River—the obsession seems unlikely to fade.

"It is in the traditional seafood stakes that the Basques really excel, their fleets scooping up spiny lobsters, tiny clams, goose barnacles, squid, sea bass, red and gray mullet, scorpion fish, anchovies, tuna, sea bream, hake, monkfish, and many others."

century resort that sweeps majestically around the bay, tucking in a fishing harbor beneath Monte Urgull and several hundred backstreet bars designed to transform your eating habits forever.

Seafood is the priority here, as Basques have always been Spain's foremost seafarers. Among them you can tick off Sebastián Elcano, the first man to sail around the world and live to tell the tale. The independently minded Basques have also produced spiritually inclined philosophers (St. Ignatius de Loyola, St. Francis Xavier), artists (Eduardo Chillida), and some of Spain's top chefs. The Spanish Basques' introspective culture, unique language, and passion for food are shared with the French Basque region that lies a

Yet there are two sides to Basque attitudes to food. Despite the accolades gained by their chefs, the general populace is slow to adapt to new trends—unlike the more dynamic Catalans, their closest gastronomic rivals. This becomes apparent in the densely packed grid of tapas bars in San Sebastián's old quarter, where, despite the abundance of tapas, innovation is hard to find. However, penetrate the more upmarket Gros quarter and you will discover innovations in the *pintxos* (Basque-style tapas) stakes.

The Basque pintxo has seen a huge renaissance in recent years. Good-bye tortillas; this is Euskadi, land of the Basques, where *k*s and *x*s pepper the language, and tapas are gutsier than the delicate French canapé. Discerning Basque businessmen are no longer seduced by homemade stew made by the barman's wife; their palates have become attuned to marinated quail with parsley oil, or smoked cod with black-olive oil on toast. The regulations for Euskadi's annual pintxo competitions state that these tapas must be eaten standing up and in a maximum of two mouthfuls. Plates and cutlery (common with tapas elsewhere in Spain) are therefore largely banished; Basque bankers are in a hurry.

The Basques have a predilection for cider; 9,513,000 gallons are downed annually in San Sebastián. A close rival is the refreshing, slightly sparkling *txakoli* (white wine from Guetaria or Vizcaya) that more often than not washes down the mountains of pintxos adorning every bar. Both these drinks are served with style, poured from a great height in order to aerate the liquid. Basques also boast a full-bodied red wine, Rioja Alavesa, produced in southern Euskadi on the borders of La Rioja province. Neighboring Navarra, which shares much Basque culture, also makes increasingly acclaimed wines, helped by its proximity to La Rioja and France.

It is in the traditional seafood stakes that Basques really excel, their fleets scooping up spiny lobsters, tiny clams, goose barnacles, squid, sea bass, red and gray mullet, scorpion fish, anchovies, tuna, sea bream, hake, monkfish, and many others. Of course, there is also cod. This was first fished by Basques in the North Sea, and soon became *bacalao* (salt cod) or *bacalao à la vizcaina*, cooked Biscay-style with pork fat, peppers, tomatoes, and onions. Today, bacalao is more of an inland dish, since fish-eating Basques opt for the abundant fresh varieties on their doorstep. Yet classic bacalao sauces such as green *pil-pil* (olive oil, garlic, and parsley) are so much a part of established tastes that they are reapplied to other foods in nueva cocina dishes and tapas.

Another spin-off from early Basque seafaring was the range of vegetables brought back from the New World. Peppers, potatoes, tomatoes, haricot beans: these are now cultivated from the suburbs of Bilbao (chiefly tomatoes) to the banks of the Río Ebro in the south.

Navarra harbors its own fertile swath of market gardens in its southwestern corner bordering La Rioja, giving it a privileged combination of basic ingredients. As a result, the inhabitants of the regional capital, Pamplona, when not chasing bulls, are cultivating the art of pintxo-sampling in determined fashion.

Food passion rears its head again in the form of mushrooms, whose proliferation in the Pyrenean foothills has inspired specialist clubs, exhibitions, tastings, and a mind-boggling range of related activities. *Revuelta de zizak* (scrambled eggs with the first mushrooms of the season) materializes on many a menu every April, while autumn favorites are wild *setas*, usually fried in olive oil, garlic, and parsley. This seasonal mania is shared with the Catalans, who scour woods and meadows for specific varieties. From these green hills, too, comes an abundance of dairy products, whether cheeses or custard tarts. Like most Spaniards, the Basques are great carnivores. Superb beef, lamb, pork, game birds, and other birds find their way onto Basque plates.

The inventiveness of new chefs is the high note of Basque cuisine. Follow their example by making some pintxos—then pile them up with typical Basque abandon and watch them disappear!

María Agustina Ostiz Baserri, Pamplona

Regarded as Pamplona's most modern café-bar in the 1930s and 1940s, Baserri is now a source of innovative pintxos. Hemingway himself would have slumped contentedly over a bar stool here between bouts of bull-running. Today, the dazzling geometry of the tiled floor and bar is reminiscent of the past, yet subtlety is the mother of invention in the kitchen. Agustina's pintxos offer an authentic taste of the region. "Navarra has a long tradition of pintxos and a strong gastronomic culture," she says, "So everything I make has to be refined and of top quality. Even if the ingredients are basic, the visual aspect stimulates taste. That comes from Navarra's strong French influence."

This doesn't mean Agustina is afraid of innovation, however. "Sometimes it's difficult to break through the traditions; I have to push people to try out new things," she says. A range of aromatic oils for selective pintxos drizzling is new to the bar. "We made them for a bit of fun and to escape the routine," she comments, looking bemusedly at the bottles that range from coffee-grain oil to chestnut or mushroom oil. "In the end, we must dedicate time, patience, and taste." You could say the same about savoring Baserri's pintxos.

Competition is hot among Pamplona's bars, and the annual pintxos competition has seen Baserri carry off many prizes, including the gold medal for Agustina's bacalao pintxo.

Smoked salmon and cheese on tomato confit
Mil hojas de tomate y queso fresco

for 8 tapas

4 large, ripe tomatoes
olive oil
a pinch of salt
1 tbsp. dried thyme
1 tbsp. sugar
black pepper to taste
1 envelope squid ink
1¹/4 cups sunflower oil
5¹/2 oz. thinly sliced
smoked salmon
¹/2 lb. queso fresco de burgos
or mozzarella, cut into 8 equal slices
4 large (or 8 small) anchovies,
marinated in vinegar

This is Agustina's favorite pintxo. If squid ink is hard to find, she suggests replacing it with a gherkin vinaigrette, which is made by chopping the ingredient and then treating it in the same way as the squid-ink oil.

1 Prepare the tomato confit and the squid-ink oil at least two hours before serving. Scald the tomatoes in boiling water for 30 seconds, then peel, halve, and scoop out the insides.

2 Cut each tomato half in half again, cross, and place the pieces on a baking sheet. Drizzle with olive oil, season with salt, thyme, sugar, and pepper, and bake for 10 minutes at 350°F. Remove from the oven and cool.

3 Prepare the squid-ink oil by blending the squid-ink and sunflower oil. Heat gently, without boiling, then remove from heat and cool completely.

4 Just before serving, arrange the pintxos on a plate by layering one tomato piece, one slice of smoked salmon, one slice fresh cheese, one anchovy (or half, if large), and a second tomato slice for each. Drizzle the squid-ink oil generously over the top.

Smoked cod, tomato, and black-olive oil toasts
(page 18)

Smoked salmon, anchovy, and red pepper toasts
Pintxo de la foto

for 4 tapas
4 fresh anchovies,
marinated in vinegar
$1/4$ lb. smoked salmon,
cut into 4 slices and rolled into
cylindrical shapes
1 red piquillo pepper (or $1/2$ red bell
pepper), cut into 4 equal parts
4 slices whole-wheat bread, toasted

for the vinaigrette
1 spring onion, finely chopped
2 red piquillo peppers or 1 red bell
pepper, deseeded and finely chopped
1 hard-boiled egg, finely chopped
$1/2$ green pepper, deseeded and
finely chopped
7 oz. extra-virgin olive oil
5 tbsp. white wine vinegar

This pintxo was originally created for a photo shoot—hence the name *pincho de la foto* ("bar snack of the photo"). The intention was to create a great-looking dish, but the result tasted so good that it has remained on Baserri's menu ever since. Agustina stresses the importance of the quality of the bread, as its texture is an integral part of the pintxo.

1 To make the vinaigrette, combine the ingredients and mix well. Set aside.

2 To prepare the pintxo, place the anchovies skin-side down and put a roll of salmon in the center of each. Fold in half and top with a piece of piquillo pepper.

3 Place each anchovy roll on top of a slice of whole-wheat toast and drizzle generously with vinaigrette.

"Navarra has a long tradition of pintxos and a strong gastronomic culture," says Agustina, "So everything I make has to be refined and of top quality."

Smoked cod, tomato, and black-olive oil toasts
Bacalao ahumado y vinagreta de tomate con aceite de aceituna negra

for 8 tapas
8 slices whole-wheat bread, toasted
1/2 lb. raw smoked cod, thinly sliced
2 tbsp. chopped chives or parsley

for the vinaigrette
1 large, ripe tomato, peeled, pulp removed, and finely chopped
5 tbsp. extra-virgin olive oil
1 1/2 tbsp. white wine vinegar
salt and pepper to taste

for the black-olive oil
2 oz. pitted black olives, finely chopped
1/2 cup extra-virgin olive oil

Another of Agustina's prizewinners, this pintxo offers a beguiling balance between the slightly sharp smoked cod and the earthy black-olive oil. A spoonful of French tapenade (olive paste) could easily be substituted for the olives in the oil. However, don't skip the whole-wheat bread; Agustina says it's crucial to the balance of the dish.

1 Prepare the vinaigrette by mixing the tomato with the olive oil, white wine vinegar, and seasoning.

2 Prepare the black-olive oil by adding the chopped olives to the olive oil and blending well.

3 Just before serving, place eight toasts on a serving plate and moisten each with about one teaspoon of black-olive oil.

4 Put a slice of smoked cod on top of each toast and dress with a heaping tablespoon of vinaigrette and a little more black-olive oil. Garnish with chives or parsley.

Fried zucchini, shrimp, and bacon bundles
Rollito de calabacín con gamba y bacon

for 4 tapas
1 large zucchini
4 strips of lean bacon
4 jumbo shrimp, cooked and peeled
salt and pepper to taste
1 beaten egg, for coating
all-purpose flour, for coating
olive oil, for frying
4 sesame-seed crackers

This pintxo is a little tricky to prepare, but once you have mastered the technique you will use it again and again. Apart from its flavors, it looks intriguing.

1 Cut the zucchini in half lengthwise, then cut four half-inch slices, again lengthwise, from one of the halves.

2 On each slice, lay one strip of bacon and place one shrimp, then season with salt and pepper.

3 Roll up the zucchini, ensuring that the shrimp stays in the center, and secure with a toothpick.

4 Carefully dip the bundle in the egg, then the flour. Heat about one inch of olive oil in a frying pan and cook the rolls until golden. Drain on a paper towel.

5 Serve immediately on a sesame-seed cracker.

Iñaki Gulin, Álex Montiel La Cuchara de San Telmo, San Sebastián

Tucked away in the shadow of San Telmo, on San Sebastián's narrowest street, is a rock-and-roll altar to Basque nueva cocina: La Cuchara de San Telmo. Through the flickering flames and clouds of steam in the kitchen, you can just about make out the toiling figures of Iñaki Gulin and Alex Montiel. These two young chefs combine culinary traditions from their native Euskadi and Catalonia, respectively, with training in top restaurants and a good dose of inventiveness. Ask them where their inspiration comes from, however, and they cite their mothers, Celia and María-Carmen, both professional cooks. "Cooks are the soul of a house," says Iñaki, "And you need to follow their example by making things with hope and affection."

Iñaki and Alex set out to create restaurant-quality food that can be consumed at the bar, quickly, and at minimal cost. As a result, the tapas are innovative and often elaborate. "We change the menu every two to three months according to the season, but we can't change everything; we must consider our more traditional customers," says Iñaki. "We may take a classic dish and bring it up to date through presentation or by adding extra ingredients. But in the end, people should be able to trust you and eat with their eyes closed." The best option at La Cuchara is to keep your eyes wide open—so as not to miss out on the next offering.

Marinated quail with applesauce and parsley oil
Cordoniz en escabeche de Modena

for 8 tapas
3 tart apples, such as Granny Smith
4 quail, cleaned, halved, and splayed
olive oil, for frying
6 tbsp. sunflower oil, plus 1 tbsp.
for frying
1/8 cup balsamic vinegar, plus a
little extra for sprinkling
2 medium zucchini, thinly sliced
1/4 cup beef broth
1/2 cup parsley oil

for the parsley oil
2 cloves of garlic
a small bunch of parsley
1/4 lb. walnuts, shelled
1 cup sunflower oil
salt to taste

This dish looks luxuriously juicy—and it is, with the quail's bountiful coating of marinade and its bed of slightly tart applesauce. The quantities here give you more parsley oil than you need for this recipe, but it's difficult to make it in very small amounts, so use it for other tapas or pintxos.

1 First make the parsley oil. Blend the garlic, parsley, and nuts in a mini-blender or small food processor. Slowly add the oil, with the motor still running. Add salt to taste. Set aside.

2 To prepare the applesauce, wash, quarter, and core the apples. Place them in a saucepan, partially cover with water, and simmer for about 30 minutes until soft. Put the apples through a blender, leaving the skin on.

3 At least one hour before serving, season the quail and brown them in a little olive oil for about two minutes on each side. In a small pan, heat the sunflower oil and vinegar. Add the quail,

cover, and cook over a very low heat for about 20 minutes or until cooked, turning the quail from time to time.

4 While the quail is cooking, quickly sauté the zucchini slices on both sides in one tablespoon of hot sunflower oil. As soon as they are tender, sprinkle with vinegar and quickly reduce the liquid. Set aside.

5 Spoon some applesauce onto eight plates, place a quail half on top of each, and lay a few zucchini slices over it. Splash with beef broth, then drizzle with a little of the oil and vinegar in which you cooked the quail. Drizzle with some parsley oil.

Tomato stuffed with tuna, garlic, and parsley
Tomate relleno de ventresca de bonito

for 4 tapas
5¹/2 oz. tuna belly, lightly cooked in oil (or canned white tuna)
2¹/2 tbsp. parsley oil (see page 21)
4 large, firm tomatoes
4 tbsp. sunflower oil
1¹/4 tbsp. balsamic vinegar

for the tomato sauce
14-oz. can tomatoes in thick juice
1/2 onion, finely chopped
1 stick of celery, finely chopped
3 cloves of garlic, sliced
1 tbsp. tomato paste
3 tbsp. olive oil
1/2 tbsp. sugar
salt and pepper

for the aioli (garlic mayonnaise)
1 clove of garlic, crushed
1 egg
1/2 cup sunflower oil
lemon juice to taste

This dish offers an unusual combination of flavors and textures—the rich tuna, fresh tomatoes, and pungent garlic are all complemented by the parsley oil. These tomatoes should be eaten at room temperature. The recipe for tomato sauce makes more than you need, but keep it in the fridge for other tapas or pasta.

1 To make the tomato sauce, put all the ingredients for it into a saucepan and bring to a boil. Turn down to a simmer and cook for half an hour or until thick. Season to taste, then puree.

2 To make the aioli, mix the garlic and egg in a small blender, then slowly add the sunflower oil, a little at a time, until the mixture is thick and creamy. Add lemon and seasoning to taste.

3 About an hour before serving, prepare the tuna stuffing by combining in a blender the tuna, 2¹/2 tablespoons of the tomato sauce, two tablespoons aioli, 1¹/2 tablespoons parsley oil, and

salt and pepper. Blend until thick and creamy. Set aside.

4 About half an hour before serving, blanch, peel, and halve the tomatoes and scoop out the insides. Fill each with the tuna stuffing and place upside down on a serving plate.

5 To make the vinaigrette, whisk the oil and vinegar together with seasoning until well blended. Drizzle the tomatoes with more parsley oil, then with vinaigrette. Add a little milk to the remaining aioli to thin it and drizzle this over the entire dish.

Creamy pâte mold
El Cremat

for 6 tapas
6 onions, finely chopped
6 tbsp. olive oil, for frying
6 slices of bacon, cut into small pieces, sautéed
1/2 cup heavy cream
salt and pepper to taste
2 green apples, peeled and thinly sliced, with the slices covered in lemon juice
7 oz. duck pâté
1/4 lb. smoked eel, in thin strips
sugar, for caramelizing

There is a mantra (see the layering order below) behind the preparation of this wondrous dish that you will probably be chanting in your sleep once you've savored the tapa. It is a work of gastronomic art, with the addition of the caramelized sugar adding the finishing touch that spells nueva cocina.

1 At least eight hours before serving, sauté the onions in the oil without browning them. Turn the heat down very low, cover, and cook for about 1¹/2 hours. Make sure the onions don't stick to the bottom of the pan by adding about half a tablespoon of water a few times during cooking. The onions should be soft and caramelized. Remove any excess oil and add the bacon and cream. Cook to reduce the cream, then season to taste. Remove from the heat and set aside to cool.

2 In a shallow, rectangular baking dish, arrange all the ingredients in thin layers in the following order: apple, pâté, apple, pâté, apple, onion, apple, eel, apple, onion, apple, pâté, apple, pâté, apple. Press down firmly after the addition of each layer. Refrigerate for at least six hours.

3 Turn out the dish and cut into squares. Dust each portion with sugar and caramelize it with a blowtorch or heat it quickly under a broiler.

FOIE SALTEADO con OREJONES
BACALAO al PIL-PIL de PEREJIL
RAVIOLI de BACON y ESPINACA
BERTSOLI de ANTXOA
CODORNIZ ESCABECHADA
TOSTA de CALLOS al ALL i OLI
CANELON CREMOSO de MORCILLA
TXIPIRON RELLENO de CEBOLLETA
CREMA FRIA de BACALAO con TOMATE
MAGRET ASADO con MANZANA
RISOTTO de MORCILLA
MORROS ASADOS con VINAGRETA
TOMATE RELLENO de MENDRESKA
CARRILLERA GUISADA al VINO TINTO
ENTRECOT de BUEY (RACION)
TXOKOLATE con NARANJA CONFITADA
SOPA de YOGUR con MANZANA

Josecho Marañón
Mari Carmen Marañón
Manuel Marañón   Bar Txepetxa

When you tire of the fantasy-laden bread slices that monopolize many of San Sebastián's pintxos bars, Bar Txepetxa will spell salvation. At the heart of the pintxos from this thirty-year-old family business are succulent, silvery anchovies, marinated according to a recipe by Josecho Marañón, prepared by his wife, Mari-Carmen, and served by their son, Manuel, who insists, "Our success lies in the hands of my mother and the palette of my father."

The small bar, plastered with photos and the odd gastronomic distinction (including a certificate of honor from San Sebastián's Anchovy Brotherhood), is packed with drinkers enjoying these anchovies with fifteen accompaniments. Each one, whether coconut, papaya, herrings' eggs, liver, or sea urchins' eggs, is laid between the fat, silver sheaths with almost sushi-style precision. What regulars avoid is the platter of plastic models, so perfect that unsuspecting newcomers reach out to help themselves. Foiled! This highlights one of the reasons for Txepetxa's popularity: the fact that every pintxo is freshly prepared. "I wanted to give people who came from the hills something from the sea," explains Josecho. "They need to taste the salt water, as well as see it." Sadly, Josecho won't reveal the recipe for his marinade, but these recipes taste great with anchovies simply marinated in vinegar.

Anchovy and trout caviar toasts
Anchoa con huevos de trucha

for 4 tapas
8 anchovy fillets, marinated in vinegar
4 slices of French bread, freshly toasted
4 tsp. trout eggs

This classic Josecho Marañon recipe is a favorite among customers at Bar Txepetxa, and it is simple to make at home.

1 For each pintxo, lay two anchovy fillets on a slice of freshly toasted French bread.

2 Place one teaspoon of trout eggs in a line down the middle of each toast. Serve immediately.

Anchovy and vegetable toasts
Anchoa jardinera

for 4 tapas
1 small green pepper, finely chopped
1 small red pepper, finely chopped
1 small onion, finely chopped
2 cloves of garlic, finely chopped
1 chili pepper, halved, deseeded, and finely chopped
a small bunch of fresh parsley, finely chopped
3 tbsp. sunflower oil
8 anchovy fillets, marinated in vinegar
4 slices of French bread, freshly toasted

This deliciously fresh pintxo takes place of honor on a plate of mixed anchovy toasts, adding a splash of color and a crisp texture.

1 Marinate the vegetables in the sunflower oil for half an hour to keep them from drying out and to leave them glistening.

2 For each pintxo, lay two anchovy fillets on a slice of freshly toasted French bread. Spoon some of the marinated vegetables on top of the anchovies. Serve immediately.

Anchovy and smoked salmon toasts
Anchoa salmón ahumado

for 4 tapas
8 anchovy fillets, marinated in vinegar
4 slices of French bread, freshly toasted
2 slices smoked salmon, cut into strips

A simple, subtle, yet extravagant-tasting pintxo. To ensure complete success, use the best smoked salmon you can find.

1 For each pintxo, lay two anchovy fillets on a slice of freshly toasted French bread.

2 Top each toast with a little mound of smoked salmon strips. Serve immediately.

Anchovy and crab toasts
Lomos de anchoa con crema de centolla

for 4 tapas
meat of 1 cooked crab, finely chopped
2 lettuce leaves, finely shredded
1 hard-boiled egg, chopped
2 tbsp. mayonnaise
2 tsp. lemon juice
8 anchovy fillets marinated in vinegar
4 slices of French bread, freshly toasted

A real taste of the sea! If you prefer a meatier flavor, do what Josecho does and add a slice of finely chopped ham to the crab mixture.

1 In a small bowl, mix together the crab, lettuce, and egg. Stir in the mayonnaise and lemon juice.

2 For each pintxo, lay two anchovy fillets on a slice of freshly toasted French bread, then cover with the crab mixture. Serve immediately.

Anchovy, tapenade, and onion toasts
Lomos de anchoa con paté de olivas

for 4 tapas
1 small onion, finely chopped
2 tbsp. lemon juice
8 anchovy fillets, marinated in vinegar
4 slices of French bread, freshly toasted
3 tbsp. tapenade (olive paste)

An intense-tasting pintxo—the one none of your guests will be able to forget! Delicious as an appetizer.

1 Marinate the onion in lemon juice for at least two hours prior to serving the tapas.

2 For each pintxo, put two anchovy fillets on a slice of freshly toasted French bread, cover with two teaspoons of tapenade, then sprinkle with the chopped onion. Serve immediately.

Patxi Bergara, Blanca Ameztoy Bergara

Since Patxi Bergara and his wife, Blanca Ameztoy, took over the family bar fifteen years ago, it has shot up San Sebastián's pintxo charts, reaping prizes for its adventurous yet subtle flavor combinations and sophisticated presentation. All the dishes meet the pintxo criteria of being consumable in two mouthfuls, but the problem is where and when to finish, for the bar is laid out like a banquet.

Not surprisingly for the Basque port and resort of San Sebastián, seafood features prominently, with pintxos such as jumbo shrimp fried with mushrooms and bacalao mixed with ratatouille and potato mousse. There is also a strong focus on the king of pintxo ingredients, the anchovy. Small wonder, then, that Bar Bergara has been chosen to represent San Sebastián at overseas functions and to fill the bellies of the finalists of the Tour de France or those of the stars at the annual film festival. The bar runs like clockwork, with Patxi filling glasses from his vast selection of wines and Blanca overseeing the kitchen.

Bar Bergara may have been around for more than fifty years, but its shelf life is definitely far from over.

Pork, pepper, and melted cheese toasts
Montadito

for 4 tapas

*4 thin slices of pork loin fillet,
about 2 oz. each*

*1 green pepper, quartered
and deseeded*

olive oil

salt and pepper

4 slices of French bread, lightly toasted

*4 thin slices creamy, easy-melting
cheese, such as French Chaumes,
about 1 oz. each*

This wonderfully simple pintxo is comfort food at its best, with its satisfying combination of pork, cheese, and bread.

1 Brush the pork and pepper with olive oil and season it with salt and pepper. In a frying pan, cook the pork and pepper until the pork is thoroughly done and the pepper is soft. Set aside.

2 Place the French bread toasts on a baking sheet. Top each piece with a pork fillet, a green pepper quarter, and a slice of cheese. Place under a very hot broiler for about 30 seconds. Remove from the heat and serve immediately.

Scrambled eggs with anchovy and red pepper on toast
Revuelto de anchoas con piquillos

for 4 tapas

1/4 lb. fresh anchovies

1 clove of garlic, minced

olive oil, for frying

*1 small can (about 4 oz.)
red piquillo peppers, drained and
cut into thin strips*

2 eggs, beaten

4 thin slices of French bread, toasted

*1 small green pepper, cut into thin
strips and stir-fried*

This dish looks fabulous, but you can make it look and taste even better by using a small pastry shell and heating it, with the filling, under the broiler at the last minute. If you can't get fresh anchovies, use those marinated in vinegar, but drain them and cover in olive oil for a couple of hours before using.

1 Sauté the anchovies and garlic in a little olive oil until tender (if using marinated anchovies, sauté the garlic on its own, then add the anchovies and gently heat through). Add the red pepper strips and beaten eggs, and stir gently until all the ingredients are mixed together and the eggs are just set.

2 Immediately spread the mixture on the toasts and garnish with a grid of green pepper strips.

Blue cheese and anchovy tartlets
Hojaldre relleno

for 8 tapas
2 oz. Roquefort or other soft blue cheese, crumbled
1 cup heavy cream, whipped
4 anchovy fillets in oil, drained and halved

for the 8 tartlet cases
1 cup all-purpose flour
1/2 tsp. salt
1/2 cup butter, softened
2 egg yolks
a little cold water
extra flour, for rolling out

Hidden between the pastry shells lies a rich, flavorful filling, so be sure to serve this pintxo with a refreshing white wine. Txakoli, the Basque favorite, is ideal, but in its absence, look for a light, dry, sparkling white.

1 To make the pastry, put the flour, salt, and butter in a food processor and process with the pastry blade until the mixture resembles fine breadcrumbs. Add the egg yolks, mixed with a bit of water, a little at a time, continuing to blend. Add just enough to make the pastry come together in a ball–don't make it wet. Wrap the pastry in plastic wrap and refrigerate for half an hour.

2 Roll out the pastry on a floured surface and cut it to fit eight small tart pans. Also cut out some lids for each tartlet. Prick the bottoms of the tartlets and chill for 20 minutes. Fill the tartlets with a few dried beans so that they can "bake blind." Put the lids on a baking sheet and cook both cases and lids in a preheated oven at 400°F for about 15 minutes or until pale gold. Cool in the pans.

3 For the filling, blend the cheese and whipped cream with a wooden spoon until smooth. Set aside.

4 Remove the tartlet shells from their pans and place half an anchovy on the bottom of each. Cover with the cheese and cream mixture and top with a pastry lid.

5 Place the pastries on a baking sheet and heat in a 425°F oven for one minute. Remove and serve.

Mushroom, shrimp, and cheese tartlets
Txalupa

for 8 tapas
1/4 lb. mushrooms, chopped
2 cloves of garlic, finely minced
2 tbsp. butter
salt to taste
1/2 cup sparkling white wine
1/2 cup heavy cream
10 cooked jumbo shrimp, peeled and chopped
1/4 lb. mature cheddar cheese, grated

for the 8 tartlet cases
1/2 cup all-purpose flour
a pinch of salt
3 tbsp. butter, softened
1 egg yolk
a little cold water

Typically subtle in flavor, this pintxo also looks terrific. Again, be sure to serve this with a refreshing white wine.

1 Make the pastry. Prepare and cook the pastry cases according to steps one and two in the recipe above, omitting the pastry lids.

2 To make the filling, sauté the mushrooms and garlic in butter over a low heat for 20 minutes. Sprinkle with salt to taste, add the white wine, bring to a boil, and cook until there is barely any liquid left. Add the cream and shrimp and continue to cook for three minutes, stirring occasionally. Remove from the heat.

3 Remove the pastry shells from their pans. Fill with the shrimp mixture and top with grated cheese. Grill for two minutes or until the cheese is golden. Serve immediately.

CATALONIA

Carlos Abellán
Comerç24

Albert Asin
Bar Pinotxo

Paco Guzmán
Santa María

Josep Manubens
Cal Pep

*T*he words "tapas" and "Catalonia" don't always mix, but "tapas" and "Barcelona" certainly do. Although the Catalans have never embraced the tapa as single-mindedly as other inhabitants of Spain, Barcelona is now transforming the habit in typically perfectionist style. This city is a world apart from the rest of Spain, an enclave of Catalan culture entwined with Gallic influences that are reflected in the Catalan language: a unique but not impenetrable blend of Provençal French and Castilian Spanish.

Dynamic and forward-looking, with a strong mercantile streak, Barcelona has reinvented itself since hosting the the rocky Costa Brava. Adrià's influence has spawned clones throughout this elegant city and well beyond, adding touches of fusion cuisine to Catalonia's vast range of homegrown products.

Eat at El Bulli and you'll be confronted with dishes of Miró-esque color and composition, such as mango ravioli with basil jelly and an orange-ginger confit—a far cry from *pa amb tomaquet* (bread rubbed with tomatoes, seasoned with salt and olive oil), the basic but delicious snack eaten by Catalan workers. Although Adrià does not serve tapas, his disciples, including Carlos Abellan of Comerç24, do.

"Designer bars dominate here as nowhere else in Spain. Inside, their customers imbibe local wines such as cava, Penedès, or Priorato while indulging in tapas and raciónes that soar to new heights of inventiveness."

1992 Olympics. Today it is a cultural powerhouse and gastronomic capital, adding additional layers to its already rich past. Designer bars dominate here as nowhere else in Spain. Inside, their customers imbibe the sparkling wine known as *cava*, or still wines, both white and red, from the wine regions of Penedès or Priorato, while indulging in tapas and raciónes that soar to new heights of inventiveness.

See Barcelona and think Gaudí. You can't miss his surrealistic, *modernista* flights of fantasy, including the still-unfinished spires of the Sagrada Famìlia temple. Taste Barcelona and think Ferran Adrià, the polemical pioneer of new Catalan cuisine, whose gastronomic temple, El Bulli, reigns supreme over

Catalan gastronomic history is markedly different from that of the rest of the country. It was on the Costa Brava that the first foreign seeds were sown, when Roman settlements held sway for more than six centuries. From them, the Catalans inherited large-scale fish salting, the predecessor of L'Escala's anchovy preserves, still rated as the best in Spain. The Moorish occupation, though short-lived, brought foods such as eggplant, saffron, and spinach, all of which remain influential in Catalan cooking today. Intrepid French monks—Benedictines and Cistercians—arrived to build great medieval monasteries such as Montserrat, but they also cultivated grapes when not at work saving souls.

The Italian influence returned in the fifteenth century, when Catalonia united with the kingdoms of Naples and Sicily. Fast-developing cuisine resulted in the first Catalan cookbooks: the *Libre de Sent Sovi* and the *Libre del Coch*. The Gallic input, first brought in by Charlemagne's army during the ninth century and long reinforced by Catalonia's geographic proximity to France, has left a notable impression on the region's taste buds.

Catalan bourgeois cuisine is known for its sauces. Many of these are based on the *sofregit*, which is composed of a typically Mediterranean blend of olive oil, onion, garlic, and tomato: all ingredients that are used again and again in tapas. Aioli is the garlic mayonnaise which, whether cold or warm, crowns many a tapa. Like the French and Italians, and unlike the Castilians and Basques, Catalans revel in aromatic herbs, such as fennel, bay leaves, parsley, thyme, mint, and juniper berries. Chocolate (added to game dishes), cinnamon (flavoring pastas or pork belly), and saffron play the jokers in the seasoning pack, confirming that Catalonia really does have a mind of its own: gastronomically, culturally, and indeed, economically.

Mar i muntanya (literally "sea and mountains"): this phrase defines not only a typically Catalan combination of ingredients, such as clams with ham or bacon with squid, but also the extremes of the region's topographic identity. Although much of Catalonia is strongly industrialized, its diverse landscape ranges from the dramatic cliffs of the coastline to wide valleys, plains, lakes, fast-flowing rivers, a huge delta, a limestone *sierra* (mountain range) to the south, and the green Pyrenees to the north. Put together, this network of microclimates ensures virtual self-sufficiency in nutritional terms.

Which is why, if you go to Barcelona's teeming Boqueria market, you can pack your basket with cheeses made from the milk of goats, cows, and sheep; lamb and wild mushrooms from the Pyrenees; tomatoes, olive oil, watermelons, peaches, grapes, apricots, and figs; Mediterranean fish and shellfish; *embutidos* (sausages) and ham from the Gerona area; and legumes from the volcanoes of Olot. The latter, a vast swath of dormant craters that is blanketed with fertile farmland and pastures, produces a range of "volcanic" organic food, some of which is incorporated into Barcelona's tastiest tapas.

Outside the market, Las Ramblas, Barcelona's heady main thoroughfare (actually five connected streets), slices down to the harbor, source of the city's abundant Mediterranean seafood. Beyond lie the narrow, laundry-strung streets of the *Barri Gòtic* (Gothic Quarter), the towering cathedral, a chunk of Roman wall, and a medieval palace courtyard. With a nod to the Picasso Museum, cross yourself at Santa María del Mar, the seamen's church, then plunge into the hip Born district, which is tucked behind Barceloneta ("Little Barcelona") and the new marina. Here, the city's funkiest young designers promote their wares; it is also where some of the most innovative cuisine is produced. Eixample, the elegant grid of early nineteenth century Barcelona, may boast architectural jewels, but it is Born that nurtures fantasy.

So when you feast on the tapas in this chapter, take time to savor their inspiration. You may well find yourself fizzing with new ideas...

Carlos Abellán Comerç24, Barcelona

Suave yet wickedly ironic, Carlos Abellan is driven by the pleasure of sharing food with friends. "Tapas is about how you eat food," he says. "It's about small portions and sharing." He wanted to put tapas in a restaurant environment at Comerç24, and it certainly offers an ultrasophisticated setting–despite Carlos's insistence that "you can feel relaxed here." At the long bar, customers perch on upholstered chairs to consume nueva cocina tapas that range from modern dishes such as basil salmorejo with lychees to traditional ones like tripe with hummus.

Carlos flies the flag of his mentor, Ferran Adrià, with whom he worked before moving on to Talaia Mar in Barcelona's Olympic Village. He subsequently spent two years commuting to Seville to scout for and set up Adrià's Andalucían outpost, Hacienda Benacuza. "I spent so much time in airports and on planes that I started devising ideas for my own place," he explains. "It took root in this area purely by chance, when I came to see friends here." Comerç24 opened its doors in the summer of 2001.

Carlos is adamant that he's not trying to do "creative" cuisine. Yet while he may express immunity to gastronomic fantasies, his customers definitely don't.

Catalan fish stew
Suquet de pescado

for 4 tapas
olive oil
2 cloves of garlic, crushed
2 tbsp. chopped fresh parsley
2 tomatoes, peeled, deseeded,
and chopped
4^1/$_4$ cups fish stock
4 medium-sized new potatoes,
peeled and diced
^{1}/$_2$ tsp. sweet Spanish paprika
salt and pepper to taste
4 (6-oz.) fish fillets, such as cod

This Catalan classic goes well beyond the quantity boundaries of tapas, so it can move up your menu to slot in as a first or second course. At Comerç24, it is served with purees of eggplant and potatoes, which are both good for soaking up the ambrosial fish juices.

1 Using a little olive oil, sauté the garlic in a large frying pan until tender but not browned. Add the parsley and tomatoes and cook over a low heat, stirring, until the mixture thickens.

2 Add the fish stock, potatoes, and paprika to the tomatoes and cook for about 10 minutes or until the potatoes are tender. Season the dish with salt and pepper to taste.

3 While the stew is cooking, broil the fish fillets, skin-side down, until golden. Serve the fish stew at once in bowls, with the fillets on the side.

Marinated tuna cubes
Bonito en sashimi marinado

for 4 tapas
1/4 cup soy sauce
1/4 cup sunflower oil
51/2 oz. fresh tuna,
cut into 11/4-inch cubes
2 tbsp. sesame seeds
soy oil

Carlos Abellan serves this tapa in a porcelain dish specially designed for such cubes, but the food's so stylish it would look good on almost anything. Make sure the tuna is ultrafresh, as this is the heart of the dish. For an even more intense flavor, lightly sprinkle either some powdered ginger or grated fresh ginger over the cubes.

1 Prepare the marinade by mixing the soy sauce and sunflower oil together. Add the tuna and leave it to marinate for at least 12 hours.

2 Thread the tuna cubes onto thin skewers. Sprinkle each cube with a few sesame seeds and drizzle with a little soy oil. Serve promptly.

"Tapas is about the form of food and about how you eat it. It's about small portions and sharing..."

Bacon-squid bundles with squid-ink vinaigrette
Ataditos de calamar con vinagreta de tinta

for 4 tapas
8 slices of cured bacon
1 medium squid, cleaned,
prepared, and julienned
olive oil, for frying
1 tsp. squid ink (or see page 15 for
substitution suggestions)
1/2 cup sunflower oil

This unusual combination of flavors is another typical Catalan application of the *mar y montaña* (sea and mountain) theme, with its squid and bacon.

1 Cut each slice of bacon in half lengthwise. Wrap two to four slices around the middle of a bunch of squid to form a little bundle, then press to seal or fix with toothpicks.

2 Sauté the bundles in a little oil on medium heat, until the bacon is crisp. Drain on paper towels and transfer to a serving plate.

3 To make the vinaigrette, mix the squid ink with the sunflower oil. Drizzle over the bundles. Serve immediately.

Roasted tomatoes with fresh cheese and anchovies
Requesón con tomate y anchoas con vinagreta de garúm

for 8 tapas

*8 ripe tomatoes, peeled,
deseeded, and halved*
¹/₆ cup extra-virgin olive oil
salt to taste
sugar to taste
*1¹/₂ tsp. black-olive
tapenade (olive paste)*
1 bunch fresh basil, finely chopped
*¹/₂ lb. fresh requesón or
ricotta cheese*
16 anchovy fillets, drained
*1 oz. pine nuts, fried
in olive oil*

parmesan crisps (optional)

1 lb. 2 oz. parmesan, grated
1¹/₂ tbsp. butter

Requesón is a fresh cheese—the Spanish equivalent of ricotta. It provides the perfect subtle backdrop for the intense flavors of the anchovies, tomatoes, and basil and olive vinaigrette.

1 Place the tomatoes on a baking sheet. Drizzle with olive oil, sprinkle with a little salt and sugar, and bake at 300ºF for 30 minutes. Remove from the oven and cool.

2 If you're going to garnish the dish with parmesan crisps, melt the butter in a frying pan and spoon on pancake shapes of cheese (about 3 tbsp. for each one). Press the cheese down and fry on each side until golden. Remove and set on kitchen paper.

3 Prepare a vinaigrette by blending the extra-virgin olive oil with the black-olive tapenade and the basil.

4 Arrange the tomatoes on a plate. Mound the requesón or ricotta cheese on top of each tomato half, then place an anchovy on top. Sprinkle with pine nuts, drizzle with vinaigrette, and, if desired, top with a Parmesan shaving.

Albert Asin Bar Pinotxo, Barcelona

Bar Pinotxo has been preparing a feast of tapas for its faithful clientele for sixty years. The stoves are now in the hands of Albert Asin, one of the five members of the Bayen family who squeeze in and out of the bar-kitchen in the heart of the Boqueria market. Watching Albert work is like watching a miracle in the making, as huge pans and woks are shifted around the stove in clouds of steam, with earthenware dishes piled above and ingredients somehow squeezed in below—all just inches away from waiting customers.

"My greatest innovation has been the wok," says Albert. "A friend brought one in and I haven't been without it since. It's the world's oldest cooking utensil—and the best!" The wok aside, Albert is a self-confessed traditionalist, yet he is not afraid of progress. "This location means I can find the best products in the market and improve the basic recipes accordingly," he says. "Good oil and salt, for example, make a huge difference."

Before Albert took over the cooking at Bar Pinotxo, it was done by his mother, María, and before that by his grandfather, Juan. Albert's father chooses unofficial customer-relations status, while brother Jordi and sister-in-law Titi transport the fare to market stall-holders.

Chickpeas with blood sausage in garlic and parsley
Garbanzos con butifarra negra

for 4 tapas
olive oil
1/2 large onion, thinly sliced
1 garlic clove, finely chopped
2 tbsp. finely chopped fresh parsley
1 oz. golden raisins, soaked in hot water
for 15 minutes and drained
a sprinkling of pine nuts
5 1/2 oz. blood sausage, fried and
coarsely chopped
14-oz. can cooked chickpeas
(garbanzo beans), drained
salt and pepper to taste

This classic Catalan tapa is the result of a wonderful combination of creamy chickpeas, sweet raisins, meaty blood sausage, and crunchy pine nuts—a truly Hispanic assault on the senses!

1 Put two tablespoons of olive oil in a saucepan over a low heat, then sauté the onion until it is just tender. Add the garlic, parsley, raisins, and pine nuts, and mix well.

2 Add the blood sausage and chickpeas and heat through, stirring all the time. Season with salt and pepper. Transfer to a serving platter, drizzle with olive oil, and serve at once.

Sardines marinated in chili, garlic, and bay leaves
Sardinas en escabeche

for 6 tapas
12 medium, fresh sardines,
scaled and gutted
all-purpose flour, for coating
1/2 cup olive oil
black pepper to taste
1 dry red chili pepper, minced
12 cloves of garlic
1 tbsp. sweet paprika
3 bay leaves
1/2 cup white wine vinegar
1/2 cup dry white wine
1/2 cup water
salt to taste

Simple, grilled sardines are ubiquitous throughout Spain, but Albert's marinade transforms them into an aromatic sensation. While this tapa is explicitly garlicky, the slight bitterness of the bay leaves gives it a cutting edge. Just as with many dishes, it tastes even better a day later.

1 At least 2 1/2 hours before serving, coat the sardines lightly with flour on both sides and quickly fry in hot oil to brown each side. Place in a shallow earthenware dish.

2 Strain the oil that was used to fry the sardines and, when cool, return it to the frying pan and add the pepper, chili pepper, and garlic cloves. Fry gently until the garlic is golden.

3 Remove from the heat and add the paprika, bay leaves, vinegar, wine, water, and salt. Bring to a boil for one minute.

4 Pour the hot liquid over the sardines and leave to marinate at room temperature for at least two hours.

5 Serve this tapa hot, cold, or at room temperature.

"What I prepare is mainly traditional, but this location means that I can find the best products in the market and improve the basic recipes accordingly."

White beans with cuttlefish in garlic and parsley
Mongetes de Santa Pau con chipirones

for 8 tapas
3 tbsp. olive oil
14 oz. fresh cuttlefish,
cleaned and prepared
1 clove of garlic, minced
salt and pepper to taste
9 oz. white (or other) beans,
cooked and drained
2 tbsp. finely chopped Italian parsley
balsamic vinegar

White beans from Santa Pau will make your tapa truly Catalan, but if you can't get them, substitute other beans. Choose ones that are as small as possible; even canned beans will do. Equally, the cuttlefish can be replaced by squid.

1 Heat the oil in a wok or a frying pan over a high heat and add the cuttlefish, garlic, and a little pepper. Sauté for one minute.

2 Add the beans and parsley and continue to sauté for one minute. Season to taste. Transfer to a serving platter, splash with vinegar, and serve at once.

49

Paco Guzmán   Santa María, Barcelona

Paco Guzman is a man on the move: now you see him, now you don't. When visible, he is a blur behind the glass screen that separates his kitchen from his low-tech bar and restaurant. When invisible, he is on his bike scouring the Boqueria market for ingredients, visiting organic suppliers, or checking out his other designer restaurant, Convent dels Angels.

Paco's Basque and Riojan origins, when combined with his culinary training in France, may give him a head start in creativity, but the greatest influences on his gastronomic style have been his Asian globe-trotting and time spent as a chef in Tokyo. Ever alert to what's in season and what's healthy, Paco's tapas menu changes regularly, and each new list, clipped to translucent lampshades above the bar, offers a sumptuous juxtaposition of ingredients.

"I decided to open an informal restaurant in which small portions of top-quality food meant that anyone could enjoy the dishes," explains Paco. Packed in the evening, quieter during the long lunchtimes, Santa María has rapidly become a foodie landmark since it opened in 1999–not unexpected, when you hear Paco describe his passion for cooking. "Mixing flavors is like playing a piano of sensations," he says. "Pressing different keys brings out tastes, textures, aromas, and nutritional balance."

Pumpkin, chestnut, feta cheese, and pomegranate salad
Ensalada de calabaza, castañas y queso feta

for 8 tapas

*6 oz. lamb's lettuce (or mâche),
torn into bite-sized pieces*
*1 small, curly endive (escarole),
coarse leaves removed and torn
into bite-sized pieces*
1 bunch of watercress
*¹/₂ lb. feta cheese,
broken into small cubes*
1¹/₂ spring onions, thinly sliced
seeds of 1 pomegranate
*¹/₂ lb. chestnuts, cooked,
peeled, and halved*
³/₄ lb. pumpkin, julienned
1 fl. oz. white wine vinegar
¹/₂ cup extra-virgin olive oil
salt and pepper to taste

The happy collusion between Paco Guzman's Asian influences and Catalonia's fantastic array of autumnal produce has inspired this salad tapa. Every autumn, chestnut-roasters take root in the streets of Spain, while market stalls acquire the Dali-esque shapes and colors of abundant squash varieties. In this recipe, you can vary or simplify the lettuce types, as the main interest lies in the balance of fresh pumpkin, chestnuts, feta, and sweet pomegranate seeds.

1 Arrange all the salad ingredients in eight small bowls (or one large one).

2 Make the vinaigrette by whisking the white wine vinegar and olive oil together and seasoning with the salt and pepper.

3 Dress the salad, toss lightly, and serve immediately.

Duck liver with sweet pears and Szechuan pepper
Higado de pato con pera y pimiento Szechuan

for 4 tapas
2 tbsp. sugar
5 tbsp. water
2 pears, peeled and thinly sliced
5¹/₂ oz. duck liver, cut into four slices
1 tbsp. olive oil
4 tsp. Szechuan pepper

Duck liver is the creamiest, smoothest liver you can get, and in Paco Guzman's recipe, it is perfectly combined with freshly poached pears and a hint of mild Szechuan pepper. Use chicken's liver if duck's liver isn't available.

1 Mix the sugar and water in a pan and heat until the sugar has dissolved. Add the pears and poach until they are just tender. Drain, reserving the liquid, and set them aside. Bring the liquid to a boil and boil until syrupy. Return the pears to the liquid and stir well.

2 Sauté the liver in the oil until it is lightly browned on each side. Arrange on a plate.

3 Spoon the pears and syrup over the liver. Grind the pepper and sprinkle on top. Serve immediately.

"Mixing flavors is like playing a piano of sensations. Pressing different keys brings out tastes, textures, aromas, and nutritional balance."

Santa Maria # 65

- Chips de yuca
- Anchoas con pan con tomate
- Hojaina de atún con cebolla tierna y aceite de oliva
- Cecina de león
- Ensalada de león
- "Rovellons" con castañas y calabaza y queso feta
- "Rovellons" con apio y mantequilla de cacahuete en ensalada
- Empanadillas de setas y pato confitado
- Ancas de rana marinadas con salsa y gengibre
- Guiso de caracoles con tortilla japonesa
- Sushi de verduras con salvia
- Maki de aguacate con salsa
- Maki de gamba y pepino
- Sushi variado y lechón rebozado
- Huevas de codorniz escalfados con pisto y chistorra
- "Rovellons botó" a la plancha
- Alcachofas guisadas con berengenas
- Tan tan de vedella
- Salteado de arroz integral con shitake, espárragos y judías
- Truchas de río con acelga, champiñones y cecina
- Bacalao con bomiato y encurtidos
- "Civet" de jabalí con manzana
- Caracltera de vedellana, col lombarda y patata
- Hígado de pato con pera y pimienta sichuan
- Al has de pollo tandori
- Surtido de quesos

※ A partir de 5 comensales sólo se sirve menú degustación ※

= Postres =

- Piña colada con chupa-chups
- Helado de caki, plumb-cake y toffe
- Manzana reineta con bizcocho de frutos secos y helado de chocolate
- Trufas de chocolate

Grilled salt cod with marinated garlic and pickles
Bacalao con boniato y encurtidos

for 6 tapas

*1 lb. 10 oz. thick salt cod fillet,
taken from the middle of the fish,
cut into four equal pieces*

5¹/₂ oz. garlic cloves

olive oil

white wine vinegar

1 lb. 2 oz. sweet potatoes

black pepper

*¹/₄ lb. pickled gherkins,
thoroughly rinsed*

¹/₂ lb. black olives

*¹/₄ lb. capers,
thoroughly rinsed*

2 tbsp. finely chopped Italian parsley

Bacalao returns to conquer, but with a distinctive Catalan twist, as its velvety texture and gentle flavor contrast sharply with the pickles. If you prefer to serve this as a main course, double the quantity of sweet potatoes and serve the cod on a bed of mashed ones.

1 Cover the cod with water. Soak for 48 hours, changing the water twice a day.

2 Start marinating the garlic the same day as soaking the cod. Peel the cloves and sauté them in a few tablespoons of olive oil until golden. Drain and put them in a jar. Add enough oil and vinegar (two parts oil to one part vinegar) to cover. Marinate for a day or two.

3 Bake the sweet potatoes in their skins for 45 minutes to an hour at 350°F, or until soft. Slit them open, remove the flesh, and mash with a little olive oil and black pepper until very smooth.

4 Lift the cod out of the water and pat dry with some paper towels. Brush each fillet with olive oil and set them on foil on a broiler pan or baking sheet. Broil until golden on top, then turn down the heat and continue to broil until thoroughly cooked.

5 Transfer the cod to a platter and arrange the gherkins, black olives, capers, and garlic cloves over and around it.

6 Sprinkle with the parsley and serve with the mashed sweet potatoes.

Josep Manubens Cal Pep, Barcelona

The bottom line of Cal Pep is its unpretentiousness: quality fresh fare is prepared quickly, cheerfully, and in a straightforward way—a reflection of Pep (Josep's nickname) himself. There is no fixed menu, as the tapas and raciónes change according to what's in season, but the dishes offered each day are expertly recited by the cheerful staff and the produce is cooked in front of you. "The fishermen only catch what's available, so I go along with that," says Pep. "I'll buy local seafood at the Lonja (Barcelona's wholesale fish market), go further afield along the Costa Brava for larger fish, and buy Atlantic fish from the Boqueria."

Pep enjoys the company of his customers as much as he enjoys the freshness of the food. "I never liked restaurants with tables—they're boring," he says emphatically, "So the obvious choice for me was to create a bar. That means there's constant contact. The food can be as good as it is in a five-star restaurant, but there's more charm and it's more fun for everyone."

Ever aware of practicalities, Pep realizes that many of his customers need to eat in a hurry. Because of the style of the food and the bar, that happens. Today, twenty-four years after opening, Cal Pep is an institution, and Pep is revered among Barcelona's new generation of chefs.

Chilled potato, tomato, and anchovy loaf
Pastel de anchoa

for 8 tapas

*1 lb. 2 oz. cooked potatoes,
very finely mashed*

1/2 cup plus 1 tbsp. extra-virgin olive oil

3 tbsp. white wine vinegar

salt and pepper to taste

16 fresh anchovy fillets

*2 to 3 ripe tomatoes, peeled,
deseeded, and chopped*

*3 oz. black olives, pitted and
finely chopped*

This deliciously different recipe makes the most of some of Spain's staple ingredients: anchovies, tomatoes, and potatoes. If you can't find fresh anchovies, choose some that have been marinated in vinegar, drain them, and marinate them in olive oil for a few hours before using.

1 Put the mashed potatoes in a bowl. Prepare a vinaigrette with the oil, vinegar, salt, and pepper, and stir two thirds of it into the potatoes. Leave for at least one hour to let the flavors infuse.

2 Place the anchovies in a shallow dish and dress them with the rest of the vinaigrette. Leave them to marinate for at least one hour. (If you are using marinated anchovies, just drain them and carry on with the recipe.)

3 To form the loaf, cover the bottom of an 8-inch square baking pan with the anchovies. Spoon the chopped tomatoes over them, and spread a half-inch-thick layer of mashed potatoes over the tomatoes. Refrigerate for at least one hour.

4 To serve, turn out the loaf, anchovy-side up, onto a platter, sprinkle it with the black olives, and cut into slices.

Clams and ham in chili sauce
Almejas con jamón

for 4 tapas
2 tbsp. olive oil, to sauté
10 1/2 oz. fresh clams, thoroughly cleaned (discard any that are not closed)
2 oz. ham, cut in thin strips
1 medium red chili pepper, deseeded and finely chopped
2 cloves of garlic, minced
2 tbsp. finely chopped Italian parsley
2 tbsp. white wine
salt and pepper to taste

The classic Catalan combination of sea and mountain ingredients features in this Cal Pep favorite. It is a simple but highly flavored dish that can easily be expanded to become a main course. Use mussels if you can't find clams.

1 In a large frying pan, sauté the clams, ham, and chili pepper in hot oil until the clams begin to open. Discard any clams that have not opened by the time the dish is cooked.

2 Add the garlic, parsley, wine, salt, and pepper, and continue to cook for about two minutes. Spoon out into small bowls, pour on the sauce, and serve immediately.

Tricky tortilla
Tortilla cachonda

for 4 tapas
olive oil, for frying
1/4 lb. chorizo or other spicy cured sausage, thinly sliced
2 medium potatoes, cooked, peeled, and sliced
1/2 small onion, finely chopped and sautéed until soft
3 eggs, beaten
salt and pepper to taste
2 tbsp. aioli

for the aioli (garlic mayonnaise)
2 cloves of garlic
sea salt
1 egg yolk
1/2 cup olive oil
lemon juice to taste
salt and white pepper to taste

You hardly know this is an omelette, albeit Spanish-style, when it appears on Pep's lengthy bar because it is covered in a deliciously thick layer of creamy aioli—hence the dish's name. Cut a slice, however, and you know you're in the realm of tortilla. If you have a small frying pan, so much the better to make individual tortillas, but one large tortilla works equally well.

1 Make the aioli by crushing the garlic with a little sea salt. Stir in the egg yolk and beat thoroughly. Add the olive oil a drop at a time, continuing to beat, increasing the stream of oil as more becomes incorporated. You should end up with a thick, creamy mixture. When you've added all the oil, add the lemon juice, then salt and pepper to taste. Cover and refrigerate immediately.

2 To make the tortilla, heat one tablespoon of olive oil in a small frying pan and sauté the chorizo quickly, until just browned. Add the potatoes and onion and stir.

3 In a bowl, mix the chorizo, potatoes, and onion with the eggs. Put two tablespoons of oil into the pan and pour the mixture back into it. Cook over a low heat for three minutes. When the omelette is firm but not dry, cover the skillet with a flat plate and flip it over to turn the omelette out onto the plate. Slide the omelette back into the pan and cook for three minutes to brown the other side. Cool for five minutes, then serve with a layer of aioli.

Curly white endive in garlic oil
Escarola al ajillo

for 6 tapas
1 curly endive (escarole), washed, coarse leaves removed
3 cloves of garlic, thinly sliced
6 tbsp. olive oil
salt and pepper to taste
2 tbsp. white wine vinegar
9 oz. assorted cold-cured sausages, thinly sliced

Pep's salad tapa is a delicious blend of hot, garlicky dressing, crunchy lettuce, and meaty sausage slices. In Catalonia, *embutidos* (cured sausages) vary considerably in shape, size, texture, and flavor, so try as many examples as you can—from salami to chorizo.

1 Pull the endive apart and put the leaves in a bowl or on a serving platter.

2 Quickly sauté the garlic in very hot olive oil until golden brown. Season with salt and pepper, remove from the heat, and add the vinegar.

3 Just before serving, pour the hot garlic dressing over the endive and toss it together with the sausage slices.

RIOJA and OLD CASTILE

José María Ruiz Benito
José María

Carlos Martínez
Meay Espinosa
Casa Pali

Miguel Reguera García
Momo

*T*ake a wrong turn in Old Castile and you might find yourself twisting endlessly through the sierra, leaving wheat fields behind, replaced by rolling hills studded with flocks of sheep, then by stark outcrops overlooking an apparently bleak wasteland. In a sweep of high plateau, the ubiquitous *meseta*, this vast region of Spain extends north from Madrid before hitting the natural mountain barrier of the Sierra Cantábrica. The name *Castilla*, meaning "castle," dates back to the ninth century, when the region—or more precisely, the Ebro and Duero rivers that slice through it—formed the frontline in

script, storks' nests atop church towers, weathered faces, meat, and more meat. There is even a breed of cow thought to be the oldest in Europe: the Negra Ibérica of Ávila.

This is also the land that produced Isabela la Católica, the infamous or astute (depending on one's historical viewpoint) unifier of Spain and conqueror of the Moors in 1492. Long before her birth, pilgrims left their mark as they traipsed through northern Castile along the Camino de Santiago (Way of St. James) in the scorching sun or bone-chilling wind. Centuries later, Catholicism and conservatism still run deep, producing a

"Here lies the heart of medieval Spain, flickering with the ghosts of pilgrims and hidalgos, characterized by gloomy bars of dark, varnished wood, menus written in stylized Gothic script, storks' nests atop church towers, weathered faces, meat, and more meat."

the long conflict between Moors and Christians. Crenellated castles rose from every hilltop, often built over Celtiberian and/or Roman predecessors.

This, however, is the twenty-first century. Although the castle silhouettes still loom evocatively, life has moved on in the villages below. Yet Old Castile (as opposed to New Castile, south of Madrid) still symbolizes a quintessential Spain—not the exuberant, flamenco style of the south, but one of austerity: silent cloisters, grains, legumes, organic meat, and velvety, full-bodied wine. Here lies the heart of medieval Spain, flickering with the ghosts of pilgrims and *hidalgos* (noblemen), characterized by gloomy bars of dark, varnished wood, menus written in stylized Gothic

firmly entrenched respect for earthy foods and time-honored methods.

Biting into the northern perimeter of this region, Rioja shares some Castilian attributes, but its personality and land are visibly richer, more fertile, more generous, and more open. The name *Rioja* is synonymous with Spain's best-known wine; vineyards stripe the undulating hills that descend to the Río Ebro, and *bodegas* (wineries) cluster around the wine capitals of Logroño and Haro. In September, the wine festival is celebrated so single-mindedly that, for several nights, Logroño's streets are jammed with carousers until dawn, all exuding a joie de vivre that may well be massaged by the vintage Rioja coursing through their veins.

Wine aside, Rioja plays a major role as northern Spain's market garden, producing red peppers, artichokes, asparagus, eggplant, and countless other shiny vegetables that tumble colorfully onto market stalls. Lamb is a culinary mainstay, while higher in the forested sierra, partridges, quail, rabbits and deer take over: all ingredients for the robust fare that compensates for the region's freezing winters.

Old Castile shares this taste for and love of meat. Chefs wax lyrical on the sensual delight of a recipe using the neck glands of lamb or that other popular tender morsel, the pig's ear. Absolutely nothing from the pig is wasted: even the hair becomes bristle for tooth- or nailbrushes. *Cochinillo*, or suckling pig, is a delicacy of Segovia, where little snouts poke over many a restaurant or butcher's counter; they are now about to acquire their own Denominación de Origen Controllado (DOC) status—a system of regulation similar to that applied to wine.

Cows are also popular, with *cecina* (cured beef) a much-sought-after product of León. The tradition of cured meat started with the Romans (*cecina* is derived from the Latin *siccina*), and for centuries it consisted of *cabbalo*, or horse, meat: the perfect chewy, long-lasting warrior food. Times and tastes changed, and beef took over, although *cecina de caballo* can still be found in remote Castilian villages.

Meanwhile, the pig continues to dominate. Salamanca is renowned for its velvety *Jamón de guijuelo*, while pigs' ears, cheeks, tripe, liver, and feet shape elaborate recipes, and the blood becomes *morcilla*: a blood sausage variously combining rice, onions, cumin, and pine nuts. Nearly every tapas bar will serve this hot, juicy, and spicy, with a neighboring plate of cold *chorizo*, the spicy pork sausage colored and flavored with Murcian or Extremaduran paprika from Rioja's red peppers.

In the realm of legumes and grains, Old Castile reigns supreme. Sacks of their multiple hues, shapes, and sizes fill specialty shops and market stalls, and menus feature countless incarnations, all dependent on the original quality product: lentils from La Armunya, white kidney beans from El Barco de Ávila, white, black, or streaked *judiones* (big beans) from La Granja, and chickpeas from Zamora. Since wheat is an agricultural mainstay of the plains, bread appears in countless forms, including as a crust on Palencia's *sopa de ajo* (garlic soup). Hardly surprising, then, that José María's highly rated restaurant in Segovia has an altar niche devoted to, not the Virgin, but *pan y vin* (bread and wine).

Then there are pine nuts and chicory from Valladolid, truffles from Soria, asparagus from Tudela, and goat and sheep cheese from all over. And in the towering moutains of Picos de Europa, which divide Old Castile from the green pastures of Cantabria, the blue cheese known as *cabrales* is made. The list is mouthwateringly endless—and so is the potential to make tapas from the products of central Spain. Even so, innovation has been slow to permeate this conservative region.

The secret of dining in this part of Spain? Get lost. Buy some wine straight from a bodega, pack a basket with market goodies, and head for the hills. Then, as night falls, make for any large town and join the throng at the tapas bars. Later, back at home, grab some red peppers, a pig's liver, or an eggplant, and re-create some of the offerings. Then uncork that bottle of vintage Rioja—you won't regret it.

José María Ruiz Benito José María, Segovia

You can't avoid the suckling pigs at José María: this is Segovia's temple to the cochinillo's delights, where some 8,000 suckling pigs are dished up annually. There's even a bronze effigy of one snuggling contentedly outside. José María himself exudes energy, warmth, and enthusiasm, despite running a staff of fifty and catering for hundreds of faithful customers every weekend. He has even cooked for King Juan Carlos.

José María is from a farming family based just outside Segovia, and developed a love of quality Castilian foods as a child. The secret of his success is his fidelity to local ingredients, which he juggles within a traditional framework, making only slight "modernist" adjustments. "The main protagonist of each of my dishes is the central food," he says. "Everything else is delicately complementary. Castilla is a serious, self-assured region, but it lacks fantasy, so I'm careful."

Despite this caution, the tapas served in José María's heaving front bar are delicious, and José María constantly reinvents his menu (apart, that is, from the suckling pig). "We try out lots of things to make interesting new dishes, but many aren't viable for making on a large scale in the restaurant," he shrugs. When he opened this bar-restaurant in 1982, he declared "I have a face and two hands, so why not use them?" The diner's response? Absolutely!

Marinated lamb and watercress salad
Ensalada de corderito lechal escabechado con manzana confitada

for 6 tapas

4-lb. leg of lamb, bone removed (boned weight)
salt and pepper
all-purpose flour, for coating
4^1/3 cups extra-virgin olive oil
1^1/2 cups red wine vinegar
^{1}/4 lb. mushrooms, sliced
6 cloves of garlic, crushed
3 leeks, chopped
^{1}/4 lb. carrots, sliced
1 sprig of thyme
3 bay leaves
1 large, tart apple, peeled, cored, and cut lengthwise into fine slices
1 bunch of watercress, well-washed, with stems removed
1 carrot, julienned
leaves from 2 endive (escarole) heads, cut into strips

for the vinaigrette

1 tbsp. red wine vinegar
3^1/2 tbsp. extra-virgin olive oil
salt and pepper

Marinades are a Castilian tradition, used for conserving fish and lean meat. The preparation of the lamb in this recipe is time-consuming and a little complex, but the end easily justifies the means as the marinade perfectly complements it.

1 Around four days before serving, season the leg of lamb with salt and pepper, dip it in flour, and brown it in a little olive oil. Place the meat in a casserole dish and add the olive oil, vinegar, mushrooms, garlic, leeks, carrots (apart from the julienned strips), thyme, bay leaves, and salt and pepper to taste. Cover, bring to a boil, and simmer gently for one hour and 15 minutes.

2 Remove from the heat, cool, and then refrigerate for three days in the casserole dish in which the lamb was cooked. On the third day, transfer the contents to a different container, add the apple slices, and refrigerate for one more day.

3 To prepare the salad, remove the meat from the marinade and slice it thinly. Remove the apple slices and mash them with a fork. Remove the mushrooms and set aside.

4 Strain the marinade and make a dressing using ^{3}/4 cup of the strained liquid. Add the vinegar and extra-virgin olive oil and season.

5 Just before serving, arrange the watercress on a plate and drizzle with a little vinaigrette. Place a layer of lamb on top, then the carrot strips, then the endive leaves, then the mushrooms, and top with the apple confit. Drizzle with the vinaigrette and serve promptly.

Marinated lamb and watercress salad (right)

Leeks with summer vegetable vinaigrette (far right)

Sautéed pork liver with mushrooms and pine nuts
Salteado de hígado de cochinillo con setas y piñones

for 6 tapas
3 young pigs' livers, coarsely chopped
olive oil
2 oz. wild mushrooms, sliced
1 clove of garlic, minced
1 tbsp. white wine vinegar
1 tbsp. pine nuts

José María prepares this dish with liver from a recently slaughtered suckling pig. However, the strong flavor means that the other ingredients can easily be overlooked by diners, so, if possible, use wild mushrooms to balance the dish.

1 Sauté the pork liver in a little olive oil and set aside. Sauté the mushrooms and garlic in two tablespoons of olive oil until tender. Add the liver and cook until done.

2 Create a mound of the liver and mushrooms on a serving plate, splash with the vinegar, garnish with the pine nuts, and serve immediately.

"The main protagonist of each of my dishes is the central food; everything else is delicately complementary. Castilla is a serious, self-assured region, but it lacks fantasy, so I'm careful."

Millennium salad
Ensalada del milenio

for 8 tapas
1 large avocado,
halved, deseeded, and peeled
olive oil
2 oz. fresh goat or cream
cheese, beaten until smooth
1 red pepper, roasted,
peeled, and cut into strips
1 bunch of watercress
4 anchovy fillets, drained of oil
1 tbsp. finely chopped chives

for the vinaigrette
2 tbsp. white wine vinegar
4 tbsp. extra-virgin olive oil
salt and pepper to taste

José María's most recent invention, created for the millennium, is a winning combination of flavors and textures. The presentation of this tapas is paramount, as it involves layering the ingredients into a tower of color.

1 At least one day before serving, place the avocado in a small saucepan, cover with olive oil, and cook over a very low heat, without boiling, for 30 minutes. Remove from the heat and leave to steep in the oil.

2 Shortly before serving, lift the avocado halves out of the oil and spread a thin layer of cheese over each. Place the strips of pepper on top.

3 Make the vinaigrette by mixing the vinegar with the olive oil, and season to taste. Form a nest with the watercress, dress with a little vinaigrette, and place the anchovy fillets on top in a diamond shape. Place the avocado halves in the nest, garnish with chives, and drizzle with the rest of the vinaigrette.

Leeks with summer vegetable vinaigrette
Puerros del monasterio con vinagreta

for 6 tapas

*12 slim leeks, white portion only,
stripped of outer layer and root
1 tbsp. olive oil
1 onion, finely chopped
1 small red pepper, finely chopped
1 small green pepper, finely chopped
1/4 lb. gherkins, rinsed of
vinegar and finely chopped
1/4 lb. capers, rinsed of vinegar,
brine, or salt and finely chopped
2 small green tomatoes, finely chopped
1/2 cup extra-virgin olive oil
2 tbsp. white wine vinegar
salt to taste
1 bunch watercress*

For centuries, leeks were relegated to support roles in Castilian cooking, but they are back on center stage, particularly in the province of Segovia, where they are extensively cultivated. In this recipe, the colorful vegetable vinaigrette that covers the stacked white leeks makes for a particularly refreshing summer tapa.

1 At least one hour before serving, cook the leeks in plenty of salted boiling water and one tablespoon of olive oil for about 12 minutes. Drain, cool, and cut the leeks in half lengthwise.

2 Prepare the vegetable vinaigrette by mixing together the onion, peppers, gherkins, capers, and tomatoes, then coating with the olive oil, white wine vinegar, and salt.

3 Just before serving, put a bed of watercress on a plate and stack the leeks on top. Cover with the chopped vegetables.

Traditional fried Segovian pork and potato
Tentempié tradicional segoviano con patatas nuevas

for 6 tapas

*1 lb. 2 oz. new potatoes, peeled
and thinly sliced
1 large onion, thinly sliced
olive oil, for frying
4 eggs
4-oz. piece of roast pork,
cut into 1-inch-wide strips
salt and pepper
4 slices of fried French bread*

This hearty Segovian dish has strong rural and wintry overtones straight from the heart of Old Castile. It traditionally filled empty peasant stomachs with an artful combination of leftover pork and seasonal new potatoes. Quick to prepare, it is more than just a substantial tapa, as it works equally well for brunch or as an evening snack.

1 Fry the potatoes and onion in plenty of olive oil over a low heat for about 20 minutes; they should be just tender. Drain the excess oil from the frying pan and continue to brown the vegetables lightly.

2 Break the eggs directly over the potatoes and onions. Add the pork, season well, and stir to mix all the ingredients together. Cook until the eggs are just set. Serve immediately, accompanied by the fried bread.

Carlos Martínez, Meay Espinosa   Casa Pali, Logroño

Halfway along Calle Laurel, Logroño's legendary haunt of tapas bars, you will spot a deep, narrow bar, usually bursting with tapas-hoppers who are addicted to the house specialty of fried eggplant. During early afternoons and throughout the evenings, this narrow pedestrian street throngs with people of all ages, types, and social origins; in all of Spain, it is hard to find a crowd more dedicated to the movable feast. As their hunting ground encompasses an easy stroll of about 200 yards, competition is hot, and the chefs are kept on their toes.

Casa Pali opened in 1994, when Carlos Martínez and his partner, Meay Espinosa, decided that there weren't enough vegetable-based tapas in Logroño. "We decided to make something healthier than the tapas other bars were making, and the eggplant became our symbol," recounts Carlos. On the walls of Casa Pali, in works of art created by friends, Rioja's plumpest, shiniest vegetable is re-created in styles from pop art to classical still life. "We're not trying to do anything sophisticated, but it's different from the usual tapas fare," Carlos admits. Try these dishes and you'll know why the bar's a success.

Fried asparagus, ham, and cheese bundles
Espárragos con jamón de York y queso

for 4 tapas
4 thin slices of mild, easy to melt
cheese, such as French Port Salut or
mild cheddar
4 asparagus spears,
cooked until just tender
4 thin slices of cooked ham
beaten egg, for coating
all-purpose flour, for coating
olive oil, for frying

The classic marriage of ham and cheese is made more interesting by the texture and subtle flavor of the asparagus. Riojans love canned asparagus spears, so for authenticity's sake, don't worry about finding the fresh variety (but use it if you prefer the extra crunch). This is one of Logroño's rare tapas that needs a knife and fork.

1 Place one slice of cheese and one asparagus spear on each slice of cooked ham, then carefully roll into a cylinder.

2 Dip the ham rolls in the egg and then the flour, then fry them in a little hot oil until they are golden brown. Serve immediately.

beicon,
queso, setas

pechuga, lechuga,
queso azul

paté con queso

Fried eggplant with cheese
Berenjena con queso

for 4 tapas

4 thin slices of tangy, easy-to-melt cheese, such as Chaumes, cut to fit the eggplant
8 thin slices of eggplant
salt to taste
2 beaten eggs, for coating
all-purpose flour, for coating
olive oil, for frying

This, Casa Pali's flagship tapa, is easy and quick to prepare. It can even be half-cooked in advance and refried at the last minute. Your guests will need small knives and forks to devour it.

1 Season each slice of eggplant with salt. For each tapa, place one slice of cheese between two slices of eggplant.

2 Dip each sandwich of eggplant in egg and then flour. Fry in a little olive oil over a medium heat until golden on both sides. Serve hot.

Ham croquettes
Croquetas de jamón

for 6 tapas
4 tbsp. butter
3/4 cup all purpose flour
1 3/4 cups milk
1 small onion, finely chopped
1 tbsp. olive oil
2 oz. Serrano ham, finely chopped
salt and pepper
2 beaten eggs, for coating
fine, dry breadcrumbs, for coating
1/2 cup olive oil, for frying

Competition to make the best ham croquettes is ruthless. All over Spain, some sad attempts and a few delectable ones are created. The Casa Pali version is a rare bird, as it achieves the perfect blend of reassuring creaminess and smoky ham flavor in a deliciously crisp outer coating.

1 Melt the butter in a frying pan. Add the flour and stir for three to four minutes, until well-blended, to form a roux. Remove from the heat and add the milk slowly, a bit at a time, mixing until smooth. Put the pan back on the heat and bring the milk up to boiling point, stirring constantly. The mixture should become very thick. Turn the heat to low and cook for about five minutes, stirring occasionally.

2 Sauté the onion in the olive oil until it is soft but not browned. Add the ham.

3 Stir the onion and ham into the white sauce and season well with salt and pepper. In a lightly greased 8 x 4-in. pan, spread the mixture to about a one-inch thickness and chill for at least two hours.

4 When cool, cut the chilled mixture into small bars, then use your hands to shape each bar into a little cylinder.

5 Coat each croquette with egg and breadcrumbs. Pour about three inches of olive oil into a pan and heat. Fry the croquettes, a few at a time, until they are golden brown on the outside and warm and cooked in the middle. It's a good idea to test one to check whether your oil is at the correct temperature.

6 Drain on a paper towel and either serve hot or at room temperature.

"We decided to make something healthier than the tapas the other bars were making, and the eggplant became our symbol."—Carlos Martínez

Miguel Reguera García   Momo, Salamanca

Opened in early 2001, Momo hums with life, with more than 150 bottles of wine and an extensive menu of hot and cold tapas and raciónes. With high-tech ventilation pipes beside chandeliers, 1950s red diner chairs, and a steel-clad bar, Momo stands out for its design as well as for its Basque-style pintxos with a Castilian accent. "I saw what tapas bars were doing in San Sebastián and Valladolid and decided to do something different for Salamanca," says Miguel Reguera García. So he joined two partners to create Momo.

    Miguel is frank about having simply adapted some established recipes, but his strength lies in his taste for the best. "I like everything on my menu, but there are things we don't do, such as tortilla de patatas—you need one person dedicated to making it," he says. Instead, Momo's menu features an abundance of cured meats, goat and sheep cheeses, leeks, peppers, zucchini, and eggplant. From these, Miguel has created designer pintxos that are dressed to kill—minimally, of course.

Red pepper, leek, anchovy, and cream cheese tarts
Queso, anchoa, pimiento y puerro sobre hojaldre

for 4 tapas
1 leek, white portion only
4 anchovy fillets, drained of oil
*¹/₂ small red pepper, roasted, peeled,
and cut into 4 equal strips*
*4 (4 inch) squares of
puff pastry, cooked*
4 oz. cream cheese

This two-bite tapa is quick to make as well as to consume, yet the pastry case makes it satisfyingly filling. The quantity of anchovy or red pepper can be increased according to your taste.

1 Cut the leek in half horizontally and cook it in boiling water until just tender. Drain and cut each half in half again, lengthwise.

2 Place one anchovy and one small strip of red pepper on each puff pastry square, then spread carefully with an ounce of cream cheese and top with a piece of leek.

3 Place under a broiler for just long enough to heat through (about three to four minutes) and serve immediately.

Red pepper, leek, anchovy, and cream cheese tarts   *Ham, fava bean, and aioli toasts (page 88)*   *Foie gras, zucchini, and bitter-orange toasts (over)*

Cream cheese and leek toasts
Puerros con crema de queso

for 4 tapas
3 oz. cream cheese
¹/₄ cup sunflower oil
2 tbsp. milk
2 slices of white bread,
crusts removed, cut in half
4 very fine leeks, cut in half
horizontally, cooked, and cooled
8 capers

The traditional Castilian leek is dominant in this tapa, and perfectly complemented by the cream cheese.

1 Mix the cheese, oil, and milk in a blender until creamy.

2 Toast the bread and place two leek halves on each piece.

3 Cover with the cheese sauce and garnish with a caper at each end.

4 Place under the broiler for one minute. Serve hot.

"I saw what tapas bars were doing in San Sebastián and Valladolid and decided to do something different for Salamanca."

Foie gras, zucchini, and bitter-orange toasts
Calabacín con foie gras

for 4 tapas
1 oz. foie gras
8 (¹/₈-inch) zucchini slices
olive oil
4 slices of French bread,
cut diagonally
1 tbsp. bitter-orange marmalade
black pepper to taste

This is an unusual combination of flavors, yet the end result is a wonderfully rich and luxurious tapa. Miguel uses *foie mi-cuit*, a superior version of foie gras with a more subtle flavor, but if you can't find it, use regular foie gras.

1 For each tapa, sandwich a quarter of the foie gras between two zucchini slices. Brush with a little oil and broil for three minutes on each side.

2 Toast the bread. Spread a little marmalade on each slice and top with a zucchini and foie gras sandwich. Sprinkle with pepper and serve at once.

Ham, artichoke, fava bean, and aioli toasts
Jamón, alcachofa y habitas con aioli

for 4 tapas
*4 slices of French bread,
cut diagonally*
1/4 lb. Serrano ham
12 fava beans, cooked and drained
*1 artichoke heart, cooked, drained, and
sliced into four pieces*
*1/4 cup Momo's aioli (garlic
mayonnaise—recipe below)*
paprika

This tapa and the following ones can be made together, offering alternative flavors but sharing the aioli topping. They are both simple to prepare, and the coating of aioli hides the ingredients for a flavorful surprise.

1 Toast the bread, and on each slice place a quarter of the ham, folded to fit the bread, three fava beans, and a slice of artichoke heart.

2 Cover each tapa with a generous amount of aioli and dust with paprika before placing under a very hot broiler for 15 to 20 seconds.

Ham, fava bean, smoked salmon, and aioli toasts
Jamón, salmón, habitas con aioli y queso

for 4 tapas
4 slices of white bread
1 slice of cooked ham, chopped
12 fava beans, cooked and drained
*1/4 cup Momo's aioli (garlic
mayonnaise—recipe below)*
1 slice of smoked salmon, chopped

Smoked salmon is a favorite tapas ingredient. Be sure to use the best you can find for this simple tapa.

1 Toast the bread, and on each slice place a quarter of the ham, folded to fit the bread, and three fava beans.

2 Cover each tapa with a generous amount of aioli, then garnish with a little smoked salmon at each end before placing under a hot broiler for 15 to 20 seconds.

Momo's garlic mayonnaise
Aioli

for 4 tapas
3 oz. cream cheese
2 cloves of garlic
1/4 cup sunflower oil
2 tbsp. milk

Aioli, or garlic mayonnaise, should always be fresh, so you should make this as close to the preparation of the tapas as possible.

1 Mix all the ingredients in a blender until creamy and smooth.

MADRID

José Angel Valladeres
Paloma Tatay
Andrés Goméz
Fernando Estrada
Albur

Luis Benavente
Bocaito

Joaquín Campos
Casa Matute

José Luis Ruiz Solaguren
José Luis

Madrid may be Spain's political capital, but it is also one of the country's youngest cities, in every sense of the word. Not developed as a capital until the 1560s by the Hapsburg kings, it cannot boast the same ancient historical tradition as Spain's other great cities, nor can it claim a truly indigenous cuisine. Yet into this growing metropolis has come a mix of immigrants hailing from every region in the country, and the population has tripled since the 1950s.

Food being a national obsession, these new citizens have brought with them their native tastes—from Galicia their beloved hometowns.

It was in the dry, electric air of the capital, too, that the cathartic 1980s' *movida madrileña*, the revitalizing "Madrid Movement" of post-Franco Spain, was spearheaded, bringing with it a sea of change in political outlook, cultural direction and freedom, and social mores. The *madrileños* readily turned up the gas in their ovens and restocked their fridges, embracing everything they had been deprived of during the long decades of repression.

Avocados, broccoli, raspberries—such foods were unknown before the late 1970s. Food diversity became an

"Go to any grocery store and you will find produce from every part of the country. Fleshy octopuses from windswept Galicia spread their tentacles over market stalls, or stew in cavernous cooking pots; fine slivers of cured tuna accompany a glass of fino sherry."

and Andalucía to Extremadura—in the form of a myriad of specialty restaurants and tapas bars. And into their kitchens has gone produce from the city's shops and markets, where a mouthwatering array of shapes, textures, and colors can be found.

Only during the last fifteen years or so have vast improvements in Spain's infrastructure secured Madrid's position as the gastronomic heart of the nation. Perhaps all roads do eventually lead to Rome, but all Spanish roads, rumbling and groaning with their truckloads of food, lead to Madrid. As a result, whatever their origins, most trainee chefs worth their salt pass through the kitchens of the capital's restaurants before returning at last to

integral part of the hot, revolutionary package of sex, drugs, and rock and roll in the atmosphere epitomized by Pedro Almodóvar's frenetic films and a string of nightclubs and tapas bars open until dawn. Like New York and New Orleans before it, Madrid became another "city that never sleeps."

Today, go to any of Madrid's grocery stores and you will find a mind-blowing array of fresh, vacuum-packed, bottled, and canned produce from every part of the country. Fleshy octopuses from windswept Galicia spread their tentacles over market stalls, or stew in cavernous cooking pots; fine slivers of *mojama* (cured tuna) from Cádiz accompany a glass of *fino* sherry; Andalucían olives glisten on every bar; and shiny Valencian oranges are juiced to frothy perfection at breakfast cafés. The one missing ingredient is the chicken egg: that tortilla on the counter is not always whisked up from fresh eggs but, instead, concocted from powdered extract. While it may be disappointing for purists, this recent enforcement of health regulations saves the population from outbreaks of salmonella during the city's sizzling summers.

Then there are jamón and bacalao, both preserved by the same methods for centuries. Armies of legs of *jamón serrano* (literally "sawn ham," but cured like all jamón and made from white-footed pigs) and its superior cousin *jamón ibérico* (from black-coated pigs), also known as *jamón de pata negra* ("ham of the black foot") are displayed behind the bars of central Madrid. The city even boasts a chain of pungent "ham museums," and jamón's immortalized eighteenth-century image, signed by artist Luis Eugenio Meléndez, hangs in the hallowed halls of the Prado.

Times may change, but the time-honored presentation of jamón does not. Pretension and artifice are unheard of: no designer packaging is needed as the truth lies firmly in the taste. Such is jamón's primordial role in the madrileño's diet that you can imagine duels being fought between the august facades of the Plaza Mayor over he relative merits of different hams. Somehow, too, the barman's ham-slicing knife seems closely akin to a rapier.

Sharing equal status with jamón is cod, whose capture has inspired many a fanatical confrontation between Galician, Cantabrian, or Basque fisherman and their counterparts from Cornwall or Brittany. First landed 500 years ago in the boats of Basque fishermen, this prized staple conquered the country, Madrid included, in its salted form known as *bacalao*. You will find its flaky white flesh fried in batter to make dreamlike puffs (whimsically named *soldaditos*—"little soldiers"), in smoked bacalao pâté or as creamy croquettes.

At 1:30 PM in central Madrid on any weekday, a crowd of businessmen, diminutive grandmothers, workmen, and lithe teenagers jostles in hungry harmony inside Casa Labra, a bar of elegantly faded splendor. The reason? This is the last source of Madrid's fresh soldaditos as well as croquettes filled with a cream of the deified food. The rhythm is regular, as large bags are filled with soldaditos to take away, drinks are poured, and mouths opened and closed over the golden morsels.

If there is one dish that Madrid can hoist as its culinary flag, it is *cocido*. This slow-cooked casserole of meat, sausage, chickpeas, and vegetables reflects the need for sustenance during the capital's bitter winters. On the other hand, you may spot a slim youngster devouring an entire cocido in midsummer—such is the madrileños' enthusiasm for this dish. A tapa that has emerged from it is the *caldo*: a cup of hot meat broth often consumed before embarking on more substantial snacks. To try it, head for the illustrious Lhardy, which has been serving Madrid's quintessential version out of an ornate silver samovar since 1839. Tripe is another Madrid favorite, producing *callos à la madrileña*: a casserole kick-started with chorizo and chilies, consumed in small portions in many a tapas bar.

The tapas on offer in Madrid seem endless, providing an instant synopsis of everything Spain produces. The next stage is to repeat them in your own kitchen—with or without that rapier.

José Angel Valladeres
Paloma Tatay
Andrés Goméz
Fernando Estrada Albur, Madrid

Young and wild at heart, the four people behind Albur share a passion for Spain's regional specialties. Being located in the Malaseña district has helped Albur become a social crossroads for young professionals, politicos, and craftspeople, all of whom mix around the long bar or tables at the back. From 2:30 P.M. onward, it's hard to squeeze in, as the changing menu is a magnet for locals, and vast portions of regional Spanish food are consumed.

"Mini," the nickname of José Angel Valladeres, is the spokesman. This ebullient man from a remote valley in Old Castile set up Albur with Paloma Tatay, Andrés Goméz, and Fernando Estrada; Fernando was the only one ever to have run a restaurant. From this team emerged a tapas menu that shifts from morcilla (blood sausage) and fourteen-month-old cecina (cured beef) from León, to cheese from La Serena in Extremadura and snails from Gerona.

"We go out and look for the best products, then order them directly from the producers, so it's much cheaper," recounts Mini. "When we opened in 1995, most of Madrid's tapas bars served Manchego food, so we decided to bring the best of the regions here. In Castilian, albur means 'making a bet' and, by extension, taking risks or being lucky," explains Mini. "In Mexican Spanish, albur came to mean 'a play on words,' so the word traveled with our ancestors, then came back transformed. That's what we are doing with our food: looking for new directions based on what exists and risking innovation. So far, we've been lucky." With imminent expansion into adjoining premises, Albur's star is still on the rise.

Mushrooms in parsley sauce
Champiñónes en salsa verde

for 8 tapas
¹/2 cup virgin olive oil
6 cloves of garlic, minced
¹/2 red chili pepper or 2 dry
cayenne peppers
2 lb. 4 oz. fresh white mushrooms,
cleaned, halved, or quartered,
depending on their size
salt and pepper to taste
1 tbsp. all-purpose flour

for the sauce
2 cloves of garlic, finely chopped
leaves from a small bunch of Italian
parsley, finely chopped
salt and pepper to taste
¹/2 cup white wine

Albur serves this tapa in a shallow terra-cotta dish—the perfect foil for the juicy mushrooms and their green sauce. It is quite delicious and the ingredients are available all year round.

1 Mix the garlic, parsley, white wine, salt, and pepper for the sauce in a small bowl. Set aside.

2 Pour the olive oil into an ovenproof casserole or heavy-based saucepan, add the garlic, and sauté over a low heat until tender. Add the chili pepper and mushrooms and increase the heat. Cook, stirring constantly, until the juice has been drawn out of the mushrooms. Season and continue to simmer on a moderately high heat for about 10 minutes, stirring occasionally, until the juice has evaporated.

3 Sprinkle the flour over the mushrooms and stir to blend well. Remove from the heat and slowly add the sauce ingredients, stirring it in thoroughly. Return the dish or pan to the heat and bring to a boil, stirring constantly. Simmer for five minutes, until you have a fairly thick sauce. Serve hot.

Mussels in spicy sauce
Mejillónes en salsa picante

for 4 tapas
4 bay leaves
salt and pepper to taste
2 lb. 4 oz. mussels, scrubbed; discard any that do not close
1/4 cup olive oil
1 large onion, chopped
6 cloves of garlic, finely chopped
1/2 red chili pepper, deseeded and finely chopped
1 tsp. all-purpose flour
1 1/2 tsp. hot, smoked Spanish paprika (pimentón de la Vera)
1/2 lb. Cebreiro cheese, or similar sharp cheese that melts well, grated

It is essential to broil this dish just before you serve it; that way, it tastes fresh and hot. Find mussels that are as plump, juicy, and fresh as possible and choose cheese with a sharp, tangy flavor, such as a mature cheddar.

1 In a deep, heavy pan, bring about 1/2 cup of water, two bay leaves, and a pinch of salt to a boil. Add the mussels, cover, and cook for about four to five minutes, until the shells open.

2 Remove the mussels from the pan, discarding any that haven't opened. Remove one shell from each cooked mussel and discard. Place the mussels in their half-shells in a shallow, ovenproof dish, pour the cooking liquid over them, and set aside.

3 Heat the oil in a large frying pan. Add the onion, garlic, chili, and two remaining bay leaves. Sauté gently over a low heat until the onion turns golden.

4 Stir in the flour and paprika and cook for one minute, stirring constantly.

5 Remove from the heat and slowly add the mussel cooking liquid, stirring it in throughly. Put the pan back on the heat and cook until the sauce thickens. Remove from the heat and mix in a blender to achieve a smooth sauce.

6 Return the sauce to the pan. Add the mussels and cook for three to four minutes. Arrange the mussels and sauce in a heatproof serving bowl, sprinkle with grated cheese, and broil gently, until the cheese has melted. Serve immediately.

Red peppers stuffed with blood sausage
Pimientos rellenos de morcilla

for 8 tapas

*8 small red peppers (preferably
piquillo—can be canned)
or 4 red bell peppers*

olive oil, for brushing

*1/2 lb. blood sausage,
preferably from León*

1 egg, beaten

2 leaves of fresh basil, finely chopped

2 tbsp. butter

2 tbsp. all-purpose flour

1/2 cup milk

*3 oz. chickpeas, cooked, drained,
and pureed*

1/2 tsp. ground ginger

salt and pepper to taste

1 tbsp. pine nuts

Spain offers endless varieties of blood sausage, but other countries are less inventive, so find the best you can. The combination of the dark blood sausage and the fresh red pepper is quintessentially Spanish, and Albur has raised this classic dish to new heights by adding basil, ginger, and pine nuts.

1 If you are using canned piquillo peppers, just drain them. If you are using raw peppers, brush them with olive oil and broil them until they are tender, partly black, and blistered. Set aside until cool enough to handle, then peel off the skins, halve, deseed, and set aside.

2 In an ungreased frying pan, fry the blood sausage, breaking it into small pieces with a wooden spoon as it cooks. Remove from the heat, add the egg, and stir until the egg has set. Add the basil and stir. Set aside.

3 In a saucepan, melt the butter, add the flour, and stir to form a roux. Cook for two minutes. Remove from the heat and slowly add the milk a little at a time, beating well after each addition. Put the pan back on the heat and bring to a boil, stirring until the sauce has thickened. Add the chickpea puree, ginger, and seasoning. Simmer for four minutes. Pour into a shallow ovenproof dish.

4 Fill the pepper halves with the blood sausage mixture, arrange them on top of the chickpea sauce, and sprinkle with pine nuts. Cook at 350°F for 10 minutes and serve.

Lamb stew
Caldereta de cordero

for 6 tapas

2 tbsp. olive oil

*1 lb. 9 oz. lamb (half leg meat and
half shoulder meat), cut into chunks*

seasoned all-purpose flour, for coating

1 large onion, coarsely chopped

*1 red and 1 green pepper, deseeded and
coarsely chopped*

4 cloves of garlic, chopped

*1/2 red chili pepper, deseeded
and chopped*

*1 1/2 tsp. hot, smoked Spanish paprika
(pimentón de la Vera)*

1 tsp. fresh thyme

1 tsp. fresh rosemary

1 bay leaf

1 3/4 cups dry white wine

salt and pepper to taste

This dish reflects the fact that lamb is still king in many parts of northern Spain. The stew could easily be served as a main dish if the quantity were increased and potatoes served with it. Note that the mixture of lamb cuts adds to the flavor and texture.

1 Heat the olive oil in a casserole dish. Dip the lamb chunks in flour, then brown them on all sides in the hot olive oil. Remove the lamb with a slotted spoon.

2 Put the onion, peppers, garlic, and chili in the same casserole dish and cook until tender.

3 Stir in the paprika, then add the lamb, herbs, and white wine. Season and bring to a boil. Immediately turn down the heat very low, cover the pan, and cook the lamb gently for about an hour or until the meat is well done and very tender. Serve in a shallow earthenware dish.

Luis Benavente   Bocaito, Madrid

Luis Benavente is one of a rare breed: a madrileño born and bred. At fourteen, he was washing plates in restaurants, his first rung on the ladder; in 1966 he set up his own tapas bar. Since then, this 150-year-old bar in the once down-at-heel Chueca district has undergone renovation and twice expanded sideways—although the original Andalucían-style decor has hardly changed. Here you will find beer from the barrel, suspended hams, marble floors and counters, signed photos of matadors, Andalucían tiles, nets of garlic, and gigantic jars of olives. Through an open hatch to the kitchen you might spot Ana, Luis's youngest cook, flinging ingredients from huge ceramic pots into the relevant pan. All these features add to Bocaito's timeless atmosphere, something that is apparent in the extensive menu of tapas and raciónes, which consist mainly of traditional or regional specialties.

"Quality of basic ingredients is the most important thing," says Luis, "Even if that means spending a little more money. From that point you move on, dressing up as little as possible." Regulars flock here from the provinces for Luis's wide choice of seafood and fifteen different egg dishes: a dying art in Madrid. Bocaito is one of the few remaining bars to serve freshly made tortillas, omelettes, and scrambled and fried eggs, whose popularity testifies to Luis's success in achieving his expressed aim: "I want people to feel at home in my bar."

Grilled lamb's kidneys
Riñónes de cordero lechal plancha

This is a classic case of the simpler a dish, the better it tastes. Buy the best-quality lamb kidneys you can find, toss them in the frying pan, and help bring them back into fashion in succulent style.

1 Place the kidneys, cut-side down, in a hot frying pan and cook until golden. Turn, coat the kidneys with their own fat, and continue to cook them slowly for about 10 minutes.

2 Season with salt and pepper and splash with lemon juice just before serving.

Kidneys in sherry sauce
Riñónes al jerez

for 6 tapas

olive oil, for frying
1 lb. 2 oz. lamb's kidneys, skinned
and quartered
1 medium onion, thinly sliced
1/2 cup dry sherry
salt and pepper to taste
1 tbsp. finely chopped parsley
1 clove of garlic, finely chopped

This traditional southern Spanish dish is for those who like hard-hitting flavors. It needs a strong wine to stand up to and complement them.

1 Pour a little oil into a frying pan, add the kidneys, and sauté quickly so that they lose their strong aroma. Set the kidneys aside and discard any juices.

2 In a separate frying pan, fry the onion in a little olive oil until tender. Add the kidneys and sherry and season to taste. Cook until the kidneys are done and the sherry sauce has reduced and thickened slightly.

3 Heap the coated kidneys on a plate. Garnish with chopped parsley and garlic.

"Quality of basic ingredients is the most important thing, even if that means spending a little more money. From that point you move on, dressing up as little as possible."

Young garlic, fava bean, and ham omelette
Tortilla de ajetes, habitas y jamón

for 4 tapas

2 oz. (about 2 cloves) tender young
garlic, finely chopped
olive oil, for frying
2 oz. small, young fava
beans, cooked
2 oz. serrano ham (or prosciutto),
cut into thin strips
3 eggs, well beaten
salt and pepper to taste

This is a flavorful twist on the classic Spanish potato tortilla, and is a dish that should always be served at room temperature.

1 In a medium-sized frying pan, sauté the garlic in a little olive oil until tender and golden. Add the beans and ham strips and stir to mix.

2 Add the eggs and seasoning and cook for three to four minutes to form a firm but juicy omelette. Cool to room temperature, cut into triangular slices or squares, and serve.

Avocado with smoked fish
Aguacate al humo

for 8 tapas
4 avocados
2 lettuce hearts, julienned
1/2 cup mayonnaise
salt and white pepper to taste
*2 oz. smoked salmon, cut into
thin strips*
*2 oz. smoked trout, cut into
thin strips*
*2 oz. smoked eel, cut into
thin strips*
*2 oz. smoked anchovies, cut into
thin strips*
1 medium carrot, finely grated
6 tbsp. extra-virgin olive oil
1 tbsp. white wine vinegar

It's hard to avoid mayonnaise in Spain, but it's particularly important in this recipe because its texture complements the lettuce, while its flavor is too subtle to fight with the smoked fish. Follow Luis Benavente's advice and buy the best quality products.

1 Halve the avocados and remove the pits. With a melon baller, form small balls of avocado and refill the avocado skins with them.

2 Mix the lettuce with the mayonnaise, salt, and pepper, and spoon a generous amount over each avocado half.

3 Place several strips of each type of smoked fish over the lettuce mixture.

4 Mix the grated carrot with the olive oil and white wine vinegar, and season with more salt and pepper. Arrange the avocado halves on a plate and drizzle generously with the vinaigrette.

Joaquín Campos Casa Matute, Madrid

In wry yet nonchalant style, Joaquín Campos hangs "The Ten Commandments of Casa Matute" outside his bar-restaurant near the Plaza Santa Ana. These are, in fact, his ten recommended tapas and raciónes—plus an eleventh for good measure. Below them he quotes from songwriter Antonio Arias: "Perfect contemplation means not knowing what you are looking at; he who doesn't know his destination accomplishes the perfect journey." With its Buddhist connotations, this sums up Joaquín's gastronomic philosophy of spontaneous and fearless experimentation. Add to this another of his favorite dictums, "Change is permanence," and you have the key to his food and to his other great passion, cinema (the phrase is borrowed from José Val del Omar, an avant-garde filmmaker and poet of the 1930s). Indeed, for Joaquín, food has a cinematographic quality: color, composition, action—and poetry.

Cultural chef he may be at heart, but Joaquín is clear about the practicalities of cooking. "I like mixing flavors," he says, "Sweet and sour, for example, and contrasting strong flavors." As a result, some of his dishes are so rich that your dining experience will stop right there, but with utter, lip-smacking satisfaction. Firing on all cylinders and a high dose of nervous energy, Joaquín is quick to point out the wines that best accompany each tapa, for the bar lines up more than eighty-five labels from all over Spain. "I'm trying to encourage people to experiment," he explains.

Although just twenty-seven, Joaquín has passed through the kitchens of some of Madrid's top restaurants. He has swung pots and pans in Segovia and traveled in America and throughout the Mediterranean. Quality and freshness of ingredients are crucial; there are vegetables from Andalucía alongside seafood from the Atlantic and Mediterranean. Somehow, Joaquín's spirited and wide-ranging approach encapsulates the very energy of Madrid itself.

Joaquín Campos

Roasted tuna served with gingered rice
Ventresca de atún confitada con arroz à la crema de gingembre

for 4 tapas

1 tbsp. butter

1/2 tsp. finely chopped fresh ginger

about 1/3 cup long-grain rice

3 tbsp. heavy cream

*2 tbsp. finely chopped parsley,
plus 1 tbsp. for garnish*

salt and white pepper to taste

*1/2-lb. belly of tuna fish,
skinned and filleted*

2 tbsp. finely chopped red onion

extra-virgin olive oil, for drizzling

The tender, fresh fish and sweet red onion are perfectly complemented by the delicate ginger flavor of the rice. It is essential to respect the baking time in order to preserve the flaky texture and color of the tuna. This dish looks wonderful on a large platter or served in small, flat bowls. If the ingredients are multiplied, it works equally well as a main course.

1 Melt the butter in a saucepan and sauté the ginger for about a minute. Add the rice, stir it around in the butter and ginger, and add 1/2 cup of water. Bring to a boil, turn down the heat, cover, and cook for about 15 minutes. The rice should be tender but not completely soft, and the water should have evaporated. Stir in the cream, parsley, salt, and pepper. Keep warm.

2 Preheat the oven to 325°F. Cut the tuna into four equal parts, then arrange in a single layer in a lightly oiled ovenproof dish. Cover tightly with aluminum foil and place in the oven. Cook for five minutes.

3 Remove from the oven, salt lightly, and transfer to a serving plate. Arrange the pieces in a ring, leaving a space in the center for the rice. Sprinkle each piece of tuna with chopped onion and parsley. Drizzle with extra-virgin olive oil.

4 Spoon the creamy gingered rice into the center of the plate and serve immediately.

Iberian ham and fava bean salad
Habitas con jamón en concha de achicoria

for 4 tapas
¹/₂ lb. fava beans, cooked or
5oz of dried fava beans
1 large, very fresh radicchio
(Italian chicory) leaf
olive oil, for frying
2 cloves of garlic, finely sliced
¹/₄ lb. Iberian ham or baked ham,
thickly sliced and cut into thin strips
salt to taste
2 tsp. finely chopped parsley

Legumes are big in central Spain, but in this recipe Joaquín Campos has chosen to limit their quantity while emphasizing their visual appeal.

1 If using fresh fava beans, cook them in a little water for anything from 2-5 minutes, until tender (the younger they are the less cooking time they need). If using dried fava beans, soak them overnight, then cover them with fresh water and cook for 1-1¹/₂ hours, until tender. In both cases, once the beans have been drained and cooled slip them out of their skins.

2 Place the radicchio leaf in ice water for about 15 minutes, until it brightens and stiffens.

3 Pour a little oil in a medium-sized frying pan. Add the garlic and cook slowly over a low heat, until just golden. Add the ham strips, heat for 10 seconds, then add the fava beans. Season with salt to taste. Cook, stirring occasionally, until the beans are hot.

4 While the beans are frying, remove the radicchio leaf from the ice water, pat dry, and place on a serving plate. Fill the leaf with the beans, allowing some to overflow onto the plate. Sprinkle with parsley and serve hot.

Duck liver in sherry
Foie fresco al Pedro Ximénez

for 4 tapas
1 cup sweet Pedro
Ximénez sherry
10 oz. fresh duck liver, cut
into 4 thin slices
salt to taste

Duck liver has a smooth, light texture and a stronger flavor than chicken liver. With the simple addition of this sweet sherry sauce, it makes an unusual and extremely rich tapa or appetizer with strong echoes of Andalucía. This recipe is quick to make and to serve.

1 Prepare the sauce by cooking the sherry over a very high heat until it begins to foam. Reduce the liquid to a nearly caramelized state. Remove from the heat.

2 Quickly fry the liver slices in a hot, ungreased frying pan for about one minute on each side, until sealed and slightly brown. Transfer to a serving plate, pour on the sherry sauce, and sprinkle with salt. Serve immediately.

Fried goat cheese with honey
Queso de cabra frito con miel

for 4 tapas

*3 medium-sized, sweet red onions,
very finely sliced*
3 tbsp. olive oil, for frying
4 tbsp. sugar
5 oz. cylindrical goat cheese
1 beaten egg
all-purpose flour
2 tbsp. honey
1 tbsp. finely chopped parsley
2 chive stalks

This is an exquisite, though rich, nueva cocina tapa. The hot goat cheese is a delicious match for the cold, caramelized onions. The honey should not be too highly flavored, as this would drown the more subtle cheese, and it must drizzle easily. The parsley is optional, but adds a splash of color to this minimalist plate.

1 Prepare the garnish several hours before serving. Fry the onions in the oil over a low heat until very soft; it will take about 20 minutes. Drain off the excess oil and add the sugar. Stir until the sugar and onions are blended and the sugar has caramelized (about eight minutes). Cool and refrigerate.

2 About 30 minutes before serving, form four equal balls of goat cheese. Dip each in the egg, then in the flour, and fry in just enough oil to cover the bottom of a frying pan. Turn carefully to lightly brown all sides. Drain on a paper towel.

3 Put the caramelized onions in the center of a serving plate and evenly space the fried cheese balls around it. Drizzle with honey, then sprinkle parsley over the top and add a crisscross of chives. Serve immediately.

José Luis Ruiz Solaguren José Luis, Madrid

The recognized king of Madrid tapas is José Luis Ruiz Solaguren, a Basque who started his working life as a shoe-shiner in a Bilbao café some sixty years ago; he now heads an international chain of tapas bars and restaurants. José Luis's gastro-kingdom not only spans three venues in Madrid, but also takes in Montreal, Miami, and Mexico City, and it has recently tacked on a vineyard and bodega in Castilla. The secret of his success? "My mother was a cook and my father a taxi driver, so I grew up with the notions of good food and service," he explains—a fact that is immediately apparent in his hands-on approach. Even at the age of seventy-four, and with two sons running the business, this dapper, expressive man still loves to preside over the comings and goings of his regulars, stopping to chat or lead customers to a table at his latest restaurant in Madrid's grandiose Teatro Real (Royal Theater).

José Luis's classic menu at the flagship tapas bar in Calle Serrano offers a dazzling range of hot and cold tapas, pintxos, and raciónes. These are good, unpretentious interpretations of Spanish classics, slickly presented. According to José Luis, "As tapas mean eating in a varied way, you can try all sorts of things, mixing different colors and textures. But the most important thing in cooking is having an appetite." It is a philosophy that remains true to his modest origins—and he continues the tradition of having resident shoe-shiners in his bars.

Ham and green pepper on toast
Jamón ibérico con pimiento

for 4 tapas
4 slices of French bread
1 tbsp. olive oil
1 green pepper, sliced
4 slices of cured ham (prosciutto will do if you can't find jamón)

José Luis serves many simple but classic tapas, and this is one of them. Be sure to use the best-quality ham, as the simplicity of this dish means it depends on delicious ingredients.

1 Lightly toast the slices of French bread on each side.

2 Heat the olive oil in a frying pan. Quickly fry the green pepper slices.

3 Place one piece of ham on each piece of toast, shaping it to fit, then position the pepper strips on top.

Anchovy and sheep cheese on toast
Anchoa con queso

for 4 tapas
4 slices of French bread
4 slices of sheep cheese
4 anchovy fillets

A wonderfully salty tapa. The sheep cheese and anchovy combine to create a powerful flavor that makes this ideal as an appetizer.

1 Lightly toast the slices of French bread on each side.

2 Place one slice of sheep cheese on each piece of toast, then top with an anchovy fillet.

Organic cured beef, caviar, or smoked salmon on toast
Lomo ibérico de bellota/caviar/salmón ahumado

for 12 tapas
12 slices of French bread
4 slices cured beef
¹/4 lb. caviar
4 slices of smoked salmon

José Luis is passionate about simple, good food. These are more ideas than recipes, but they make luxuriously simple snacks and look great on a plate together.

1 Lightly toast the slices of French bread on each side.

2 Place slices of the best-quality cured beef on four pieces of toast, a heaping spoonful of caviar on the next four, and a slice of smoked salmon on each of the remaining pieces.

Smoked fish tartar
Tartar de ahumados

for 4 tapas

4 slices of French bread
*2 oz. smoked anchovies,
finely chopped*
*2 oz. smoked salmon,
finely chopped*
*2 oz. smoked trout,
finely chopped*
2 tsp. diced onion
2 tsp. diced capers
3 oz. mayonnaise

A delicious combination of three types of smoked fish, this is another salty tapa that makes a terrific appetizer. The onion and capers add a piquancy that will really set your mouth watering.

1 Lightly toast the slices of French bread on each side.

2 Mix the smoked anchovies, salmon, and trout together. Add the chopped onion and capers and blend well. Mix in the mayonnaise.

3 Heap a large spoonful of the paste onto each toast, and serve.

"As tapas mean eating in a varied way, you can try all sorts of things, mixing different colors and textures. But the most important thing in cooking is having an appetite."

Esteban Miñana
La Bodeguilla del Gato

Colin Ward
Gambrinus

Emiliano García Domene
Bodega Montaña

Michele Gallana
Santa Companya

Raquel Sabater
Mesón de Labradores

"*T*he land where the east wind blows": this is Spain's Levante, and the phrase carries a revealing echo of the region's gastronomic influences from the Middle East. Between the beaches and the herb-studded sierra, this Mediterranean coastal region produces an astonishingly abundant and diverse range of food.

Not quite milk and honey, more rice and oranges, the Levante's produce encompasses glistening fish, almonds, cherries, grapes, grapefruit, lemons, loquats, artichokes, black truffles, dates, and, yes, honey. Rich soil, a temperate climate, and a history of multifarious agricultural influences give the region the

restaurants during protracted family get-togethers every Sunday. Alongside the fragrant, saffron-imbibed amalgam of chicken, shrimp, vegetables, and rice (a dish that has, sadly, suffered an abusive, tourist-oriented fate), paella's many variations may combine bacalao with spinach, or rabbit with seafood, and may include either small game, turkey, or sausage meats. And, despite its association with gargantuan proportions, paella is sometimes spooned out at bars in tapa-sized portions—both in the Levante and in other regions of Spain.

Of course, the heart and soul of any paella is rice, although even this is

"Not quite milk and honey, more rice and oranges, the Levante's produce encompasses glistening fish, almonds, cherries, grapes, grapefruit, loquats, artichokes, black truffles, dates, and, yes, honey."

reputation of being the most fertile in the whole of Europe. This, along with the Levante's ability to attract a rather cosmopolitan population, are the key influences behind the area's "new" tapas.

Paella, Spain's national dish, was born near Valencia, the Levante's main city, barely two centuries ago. As is often the case with dishes that make such imaginative use of some basic ingredients, paella evolved from the poor man's needs, combining tasty leftovers into a body-building lunch that, conveniently, could be prepared outdoors over an fire.

The tradition of never eating paella in the evening continues, in order to accommodate digestion, but more often than not, this dish is now consumed in

sometimes replaced by *fideos* (fine noodles that will absorb squid ink, saffron, or fish-juices). Rice, whether grains of *bomba*, *granza*, or *secreti*, was first cultivated here by the Moors during their 500-year rule over the region, and paddy fields still blanket the marshes surrounding the Albufera lagoon, south of Valencia. Evidence of the grain's versatility and inspirational role is that one restaurant in Alicante features as many as seventy rice dishes on its menu.

Before the Moors, the equally long Roman occupation left a taste in this region for seafood preserved in brine or salt, while waves of Jewish settlers brought with them luscious Middle Eastern influences. Even longer ago than that, salt was produced by the Iberians in the salt marshes of Murcia, to the south, while the palm grove at Elche—now Europe's largest, with as many as 125,000 date palms—is thought to have been planted by the Phoenicians.

The Italian influence upon food, art, and architecture returned in the fifteenth and sixteenth centuries, when Spain's eastern seaboard governed Naples and Sicily. Yet the Levante's resultant mercantile glory foundered once the *Moriscos* (Moors converted to Christianity) and Jews were turned out in 1609. With this exodus of both traders and skilled farmers, the backbone of agriculture in the region fell apart, to be revived only in more recent years.

One spin-off of the Levante's abundance is that the diet enjoyed in the area is arguably the most balanced in all of Spain. Fish is the mainstay, along with rice *a banda* (cooked in fish broth and served separately) and heaps of roasted vegetables (*escalibada*), which are liberally doused in olive oil, followed by the juiciest-possible seasonal fruit. Valencian dessert foods reflect the region's Arab influence: *horchata* (a cold drink made from the *chufa*, or tiger nut, a peanut-sized tuber), almonds, honey, and candied fruitcakes abound, alongside marzipan and *turrón* (nougat).

In cultural terms, contemporary Valencia is speeding swiftly ahead, incorporating flashes of designer chic into a city of stunning Renaissance buildings whose towering cathedral claims to possess the Holy Grail, no less, in its museum. As the Valencian identity strengthens, its protagonists separate themselves increasingly from their Catalan cousins to the north of the country—people who, although speaking a language similar to that of the Valencians, have notable historical and social differences.

You can sense the ongoing renewal in Valencia as you wander through grandiose squares lined with renovated mansions, enter a converted convent that is now a contemporary arts center, or survey the expanding forms of Santiago Calatrava's ambitious City of Arts and Sciences. The growing cosmopolitanism is evident on a more basic level, for here you can sip a good Australian wine while enjoying an Italian tapa in one of the city's ever-increasing number of specialty tapas bars.

As in Catalonia, the tapas tradition is not as deeply embedded in Valencia as it is in Madrid, Andalucía, or the Basque Country. However, in the narrow streets of the old quarter of Valencia, entrepreneurial young chefs from Bilbao, Venice, and London are setting a different tone for this metamorphosing city. It would not be difficult to bet that, within just a few years, it will vie with Barcelona and Madrid as a destination for food-lovers.

Despite these changes, there remains something touchingly Old World about Valencia, whether in the last decoratively peeling facades, in the shops overflowing with *mantillas* (scarves), fans, and embroidered shawls; in a tiled bar with neon tubes artfully inserted into an aging chandelier; or in the succulent anchovies that are sold by the single fillet.

Above all, the magnificent iron and glass creation that is the seventy-five-year-old Mercado Central, one of Europe's most fantastic and diverse municipal markets, paints the true picture of the Levante's gastronomic riches. Valencia is not globalized—yet. It is human, for the moment, at any rate. Follow this region's example by concentrating on astute combinations of ultrafresh ingredients and your taste buds, as well as your constitution, will be grateful.

Esteban Miñana   La Bodeguilla del Gato, Valencia

Located in the heart of El Carmen, a hot, nocturnal quarter (hence Gato–"cat," which refers to the nocturnal habits of the madrileños), this tapas bar brings with it influences and traditions from northern Spain. On the menu, developed by chef Estéban Miñana and owners Pepe Lopez and Andres Canelas, are tapas that wouldn't look out of place in Bilbao or Madrid, the trio's original home ground.

Estéban notes that there is a big difference in tapas-eating habits in the north and south of Spain. "Here," he explains, "people tend to sit and eat, drinking cocktails or beer, whereas in the north they move around from bar to bar, drinking copas (glasses) of wine. It means that tapas have actually become a meal here." Estéban's first career as an industrial designer also influences his approach. "Food and design are both about a mixture of colors and lines," he says. "Taste is, of course, important, but appearance counts, too." Make no mistake, however: Estéban's unpretentious classics are full of flavor.

Open only in the evenings, La Bodeguilla del Gato packs in its ravenous customers between brick walls hung with contemporary paintings, photographs of bullfighting, and concert posters. Despite–or perhaps because of–their northern influence, Estéban's tapas obviously appeal to local appetites.

Fishermen's mussels
Mejillónes à la marinera

for 8 tapas

1 lb. 10 oz. fresh mussels, scrubbed,
any open ones discarded
about 1/3 cup dry white wine
1 bay leaf
2 tbsp. olive oil
1 large onion, finely chopped
1 red pepper, finely chopped
1 green pepper, finely chopped
2 cloves of garlic, finely chopped
2 ripe tomatoes, finely chopped
a pinch of cayenne pepper
white pepper to taste

Choose large, plump mussels to complement the generous tomato sauce with its aromatic echoes of the Mediterranean.

1 Place the mussels in a large pot with the wine and bay leaf, and cook, covered, over a high heat for a few minutes, shaking occasionally, until all the shells have opened (discard any that do not). Transfer the mussels to a serving platter and keep them warm. Reserve the cooking liquid.

2 Heat the olive oil in a saucepan. Sauté the onion, peppers, and garlic until tender. Add the tomatoes and cayenne pepper and cook for about 15 minutes, until the mixture is thick. Stir in a little of the cooking liquid and season with white pepper.

3 Pour the sauce over the mussels and serve at once.

Spicy sausage in red wine
Chorizo al vino

for 4 tapas

*1 lb. 4 oz. chorizo or
other spicy sausage*
1 1/2 cups dry red wine
1 bay leaf

In the north of Spain, chorizo is often cooked in cider. Estéban prefers to adapt the recipe, using red wine instead of cider to create a warmer dish. This makes an excellent wintry tapa to accompany glasses of good Rioja.

1 Place the sausage in a frying pan with the wine and bay leaf. Cover and cook over a low heat for 10 to 15 minutes, or until the wine has been slightly reduced.

2 Remove the sausage from the pan and cut it into half-inch slices. Return the slices to the wine and stir. Serve in individual earthenware dishes with chunks of French bread.

Squid in tomato and garlic sauce
Sepia encebollada

for 4 tapas

*1 lb. 9 oz. squid, cleaned, prepared,
and cut into 1-inch pieces*
1/2 cup water
1 bay leaf
4 cloves of garlic, thinly sliced
olive oil, for frying
1 large onion, thinly sliced in rings
1 ripe tomato, finely chopped
1/2 tbsp. paprika
1 glass white wine or 1/2 glass cognac
salt and pepper to taste

This is a classic Mediterranean dish, combining squid with some of the region's favorite ingredients: tomatoes, onions, garlic, and bay leaves. Use cognac instead of white wine for a more intense sauce.

1 Place the squid in a heavy cooking pot with the water and bay leaf. Bring to a boil and boil for three minutes, while stirring constantly to separate the pieces of squid. Remove from the pot; set aside. Reserve the cooking liquid.

2 Sauté the garlic in a little olive oil until tender. Add two more tablespoons of olive oil and the onion rings. Cover and cook over a low heat for about 20 minutes.

3 Add the tomato, paprika, white wine or cognac, salt, and pepper. Cook slowly, uncovered, until the sauce is quite thick. Add the squid and some of the cooking liquid to the sauce and stir to mix well. Serve immediately.

SEPIA

250 Ptas 1/4 Kg

1000 Ptas Kilogramo

Colin Ward — Gambrinus, Valencia

*This could be the joker in our pack. A Londoner held up as an exemplary conjuror of tapas?
Yet somehow Gambrinus—situated in the Plaza de la Reina, Valencia's most illustrious square—
is quintessentially Spanish. It nets large family groups for Sunday paella and a constant flow
during the rest of the week for its succulent tapas. In the summer, the overflow is
accommodated by outdoor tables from which diners can muse on the Gothic cathedral,
its octagonal bell tower, and the truth behind its Holy Grail.*

*The success of Gambrinus's food owes much to chef Colin Ward's Andalucían adolescence,
when, between fruit-picking, cultivating his own vegetable garden, and dodging errant
donkeys, he developed a passion for all things Spanish. "When I went back to London, I
became a singer in a band that came to Valencia for a few gigs," he recalls. "Then I met my
Mallorcan wife, and so the die was cast and we came here to live." Colin has since mastered
a repertoire of Valencian dishes and tapas that no local chef could criticize. "In the end," he
says, "Valencian food is all about fresh ingredients, and the local pork and chicken are
particularly good. You don't need sauces to hide anything, as the basic flavors are all there."*

*There's a personal angle to at least one of Colin's dishes, too, as he readily confesses:
"The pica-pica recipe I learned from my wife, who learned it from her grandmother."*

Tarragon chicken with asparagus
Pollo al estragón

for 4 tapas
4 tbsp. butter
1 medium onion, finely chopped
1/2 lb. chicken breast,
cut into 1-inch cubes
about 2-3 tbsp. chopped,
fresh tarragon leaves
4 tbsp. all-purpose flour
1 1/2 cups milk
8 stalks fresh asparagus, peeled and
coarsely chopped
salt and pepper to taste

Asparagus grows prolifically in Valencia, but while it may be a traditional ingredient, milk–a food rarely seen in Spanish cooking–is definitely much more English. But then this is cosmopolitan Valencia, so why not?

1 Melt the butter in a large frying pan. Add the onion and chicken and cook, stirring frequently, until the onion is tender and the chicken is lightly browned. Add the tarragon and flour and cook gently, stirring until well mixed. Take the pan off the heat and slowly add the milk, blending in each addition before adding more. Put the pan back on the heat and bring to a boil, stirring constantly, until the mixture has thickened and is smooth and creamy.

2 Turn down the heat, add the asparagus, salt, and pepper, and simmer for 5 minutes or until the chicken is thoroughly cooked. Serve hot in individual earthenware dishes.

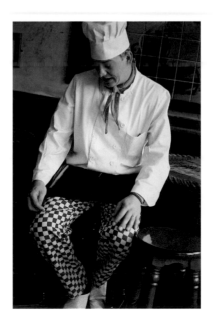

Marinated mackerel with roasted vegetables
Escalibada con caballa en escabeche

for 6 tapas

1 eggplant, halved lengthwise
1 zucchini, halved lengthwise
1 onion, peeled and quartered
1 red pepper, halved and deseeded
1 fennel bulb, trimmed, quartered, and heart removed
olive oil, for roasting
ground rock salt to taste
1/2 cup dry white wine
1 cup olive oil
4 mackerel fillets
6 cloves
4 cloves of garlic, unpeeled
4 bay leaves

Escalibada is an eastern Spanish classic that makes full use of the abundant fresh vegetables grown locally. The name comes from the Catalan word for "charred," and ideally the vegetables should be cooked over a barbecue to get a really full, smoky flavor. Escalibada can be served with any kind of preserved or marinated fish, though mackerel works perfectly.

1 Place the vegetables (except for the garlic) cut-side down on a baking sheet, brush with olive oil, season with rock salt, and roast at 400°F for 35 minutes. Remove from the oven and set aside.

2 For the marinade, whisk together the wine and olive oil. Put the mackerel fillets in a wide saucepan and pour over just enough marinade to cover them. Add the cloves, garlic, and bay leaves, cover, and simmer for 15 minutes.

3 Peel the skin from the roast pepper halves and cut the stem off the eggplant halves. Slice the vegetables thinly and arrange in the center of a plate. Place the mackerel fillets on top of the vegetables and garnish the rim of the plate with the bay leaves and garlic cloves. This tapa can be served warm or cool, but not refrigerated.

Squid in tomato, garlic, and red wine sauce
Calamares pica-pica

for 4 tapas
¹/₂ cup olive oil
*1 lb. 2 oz. squid, cleaned
and cut into 2-inch pieces*
1 onion, coarsely chopped
¹/₂ lb. tomatoes, coarsely chopped
2 cloves of garlic, crushed
1 red pepper, coarsely chopped
1 bay leaf
1 cup red wine
¹/₂ cup fish stock

Easy to make yet oozing with flavor, this Mallorcan tapa is a real hit in Valencia. Make sure the squid you use is small and tender.

1 Heat the olive oil in a large saucepan. Add the squid and stir-fry for one minute. Add the onion and tomatoes and fry for five minutes.

2 Add the garlic, pepper, bay leaf, red wine, and stock. Stir, then simmer for 20 minutes. Serve hot in earthenware dishes with crusty bread.

Cod, spinach, and tomato paella
Paella de bacalao y espinacas

for 6 tapas

*1 lb. 2 oz. fresh spinach, washed,
stalks removed*
4 tbsp. olive oil
*6 oz. salt cod, desalted (see page 58,
step 1) and cut into strips*
2 tbsp. pine nuts
1/2 lb. tomatoes, chopped
2 cloves of garlic, crushed
2 tsp. paprika
1 dried chili pepper, chopped
1/2 lb. Calasparra rice
2 1/4 cups vegetable stock
*1/2 tsp. saffron threads, infused in
2 tbsp. of boiling water for 15 minutes*
salt to taste
lemon wedges to serve

Of the myriad of forms of paella, this is one of the most delicious, with its distinctive flavor and dark color. You can replace the salt cod with fresh cod, but try to use small, round-grained Spanish Calasparra rice, particularly the kind known as *bomba*.

1 In a covered saucepan, using only the water left on the leaves after washing, cook the spinach over a medium heat for four minutes. Squeeze out the excess water and chop.

2 Heat the oil in a large frying pan. When very hot, add the cod, spinach, pine nuts, tomatoes, garlic, paprika, and dried chili. Lower the heat and cook, stirring constantly, for six minutes.

3 Add the rice and continue to cook, stirring constantly, for two minutes. Add the stock and saffron. Season with salt and simmer for about 15 minutes or until the stock has been absorbed and the rice is just tender.

4 Remove from the heat, cover with a dishcloth, put the lid on, and allow to stand for five minutes. Garnish with lemon wedges and serve at once.

Emiliano García Domene   Bodega Montaña, Valencia

The Mediterranean plays a key role in the tapas at Bodega Montaña, not least because the bar lies just a few blocks from the waves in El Cabañal, the fishermen's quarter on the outskirts of Valencia. Despite its remote location, Bodega Montaña's well-worn features (it dates from 1836), list of more than 900 wines, and succulent tapas ensure that it is known by every self-respecting tapas-hopper in the city. Serving them all is Vicente, the well-disposed manager.

From its modest early days as a general store, Bodega Montaña blossomed under the forty-five-year ownership of a Frenchman who introduced wine, olive oil, and finally, tapas. When Emiliano García Domene took over in the early 1990s, he introduced wines from Italy, Argentina, Chile, New Zealand, Australia, and South Africa to accompany the stocks of Rioja and Valdepeñas. For Spain—and even more so for Valencia—this was a brave step.

And the tapas? Again, concentrating on quality products but respecting local tastes, the menu offers the classics: a wide variety of specialty sausages and hams and a string of seafood delicacies. Premium anchovy fillets are sold individually, while Valencian clochinas (mussels), sardines, squid, and octopus are the standard delectable fare.

Mashed potatoes, salt cod, and garlic
Bacalao al ajo arriero

for 6 tapas

1 lb. 2 oz. peeled potatoes
3 hard-boiled egg yolks, chopped
4 large cloves of garlic, finely chopped
1/2 lb. salt cod, desalted (see
page 58, step 1) and finely chopped
1/2 cup olive oil

This delicious little tapa is served packed into tiny dishes with a breadstick pushed into one end. It's an easy, basic dish that your guests will devour without noticing. The quantities below are generous, catering to fishermen's appetites.

1 Boil the potatoes until just soft. Remove from the heat, drain, and then mash them. Once mashed, beat them with a wooden spoon to ensure they are smooth.

2 Add the egg yolks, garlic, and cod. Mix well, and continue to beat briskly while slowly adding the olive oil. Beat into a smooth, thick puree. Serve as a dip for crackers or breadsticks.

Deep-fried red piquillo peppers with tuna stuffing
Pimientos del piquillo rellenos

for 4 tapas
8 whole red piquillo peppers, fresh or
canned, or 4 red bell peppers
2 tbsp. butter
1 tbsp sunflower oil
about 2 tbsp. all-purpose flour
a pinch of cornstarch
1¼ cups milk
salt and pepper to taste
freshly grated nutmeg to taste
6 oz. canned tuna in oil, drained
and flaked
1 beaten egg, for coating
all-purpose flour, for coating
olive or sunflower oil, for frying

Although piquillo peppers are grown in Navarra and Rioja, they are in demand throughout the country for their concentrated juiciness and sweetness. If you can't find fresh ones, use the canned variety.

1 If using fresh peppers, halve and deseed them, then broil until blistered and black in places. Leave them to cool, then peel off the skin.

2 To prepare the stuffing, make a white sauce by melting the butter in a pan with the sunflower oil. Add the flour and cornstarch, stirring constantly until the flours and fats come together and make a roux. Cook until the roux is pale gold, then remove from the heat. Add the milk, a little at a time, stirring well after each addition. Put the pan back on the heat and bring to a boil, stirring constantly to make a smooth sauce. Cook over a low heat, stirring from time to time, for five minutes.

3 Take the sauce off the heat and season well with salt, pepper, and nutmeg. Add the tuna and mix thoroughly, then allow to cool. Refrigerate for 12 hours.

4 About half an hour before serving, fill the peppers with the tuna mixture, being careful not to tear them. Fold over the filling. Dip the stuffed peppers in the egg, then in the flour and then carefully lower them into the hot oil with the slotted spoon. Fry in about four inches of hot oil until lightly browned on all sides. Drain on paper towels and serve immediately.

Artichoke hearts with black-olive oil
Alcachofa con aceite de oliva negra

for 8 tapas
¹/₂ lb. pitted black olives
¹/₂ cup extra-virgin olive oil
8 artichoke hearts, cooked, or canned
and well-drained

Bar Montaña has produced an ultrasimple recipe here that is light and delicious, yet looks like a work of art.

1 Prepare the black-olive oil by mixing the olives and oil in a blender until the olives are finely chopped.

2 Just before serving, place the artichoke hearts on a plate and pour the black-olive oil over them.

Spicy fava bean and pork stew
Habas condimentadas

for 6 tapas
1 lb. 2 oz. dried fava beans, soaked
for 48 hours
1 oz. lomo ibérico (cured pork loin)
1 oz. cured beef
2 oz. chorizo or other
spicy sausage
1 oz. smoked ham
1 small ham bone
¹/₄ lb. chistorra or pork sausage
a handful (about 1 oz.) fresh mint leaves
6 bay leaves
1 tsp. cayenne pepper
7 cups chicken stock
or water
4 tbsp. olive oil
about 2 tbsp. hot, smoked Spanish
paprika (pimentón de la Vera)
salt and pepper to taste

Typical of southern Spanish peasant food, this tapa contrasts the satisfying earthiness of pork and other meats with the mellow fava beans—a legume that definitely deserves a revival.

1 In a large saucepan, place all the ingredients (except the olive oil, paprika, and salt) in the order in which they appear in the ingredients list, then use just enough stock or water to cover.

2 Heat the olive oil in a small frying pan, add the paprika, and stir until well blended. Pour this over the bean mixture, cover the pan, and place on a high heat. When the mixture comes to a boil, turn down the heat and cook slowly for one to two hours or until the beans are tender. Top off with extra stock from time to time, if necessary.

3 Remove the ham bone. Season the stew with salt and pepper (adding salt before this stage would make the beans hard), and serve hot in individual earthenware dishes.

Michele Gallana   Santa Companya, Valencia

Food fans beware: this hip bar, hidden in central Valencia's maze of narrow streets, is breaking new fusion ground. And that's fusion in the Mediterranean sense, as opposed to East-West. Santa Companya was opened in 2001 by a young Italian architect, Michele Gallana, two silent partners, both of whom are Italian, and a Valencian architect who designed the bar. All the tapas and raciónes are prepared at a tiny counter behind the bar, where much attention is paid to presentation, as well as to taste. The bar only serves chilled dishes, from open sandwiches (montaditos) of specialty European cheeses (Gorgonzola, St. Nectaire, Stilton) with honey, marmalade, or quince paste, to tapas based on Spanish and Italian sausages, Galician seafood preserves, or epicurean salads. Loaves and fishes eat your heart out: Italian savoir-faire has hit town. Michele hails from the Veneto. "My grandmother had a restaurant that I often went to as a child," he says. "We opened this wine bar to serve top-quality European wines." Food was not the original priority, but the momentum grew, and customers now come as much for the ricotta or Parma ham as for the Rioja. "Valencians stay longer in bars than people elsewhere in Spain. They order a bottle, not a glass, and they sit," Michele says. This is an excellent reason for imitating Santa Companya's success by following his recipes.

Ostrich carpaccio
Carpaccio de avestruz

for 4 tapas
1/2-lb. ostrich (or beef) fillet, cooked and cut into paper-thin slices
1/2 cup olive oil, for the marinade
several fresh mint leaves
peel from one mandarin orange, cut into small pieces
about 1/3 cup whole-grain Dijon mustard
juice of half an orange
1-2 tbsp. olive oil, for the sauce
salt and pepper to taste
6 drops of 8-year-old balsamic vinegar
2 tbsp. almond slivers
2 tbsp. pine nuts

Although Michele developed this recipe for ostrich meat, it is equally good with beef. The virtually transparent slices of meat easily absorb the tangy orange and mint flavors. Combined with the flavors of mustard and balsamic vinegar, this makes a highly aromatic and easily devoured tapa.

1 Marinate the ostrich in the olive oil, mint leaves, and orange peel for one hour.

2 For the sauce, mix the mustard, orange juice, olive oil, salt, and pepper.

3 Remove the meat from the marinade and arrange it on a platter. Cover with the sauce, sprinkle with the vinegar, and garnish with the almond slivers and pine nuts.

Spicy steak tartar
Bistec tartar de Michele

for 6 tapas
4 tbsp. finely chopped parsley
4 mild chili peppers, deseeded and finely chopped
1 small onion, finely chopped
2 oz. capers, well rinsed
1 lb. 2 oz. sirloin steak, finely chopped
6 drops hot-pepper sauce
salt and pepper to taste
extra-virgin olive oil to taste
1/4 cup Dijon herb mustard

The palate is under a happy assault from this spicy tapa, with its fiery mix of onion, chilies, capers, and hot-pepper sauce.

1 In a bowl, mix together the parsley, chilies, onion, and capers. Add the finely chopped sirloin and mix well.

2 Sprinkle with hot-pepper sauce, salt, pepper, and oil and mix to combine all the ingredients. Heap on a platter or on individual plates and serve with the herb mustard.

Marinated sardines with onions in sherry
Sarde en Saor

for 6 tapas
1 lb. 2 oz. small, fresh sardines, gutted and scaled
all-purpose flour for coating
olive oil, for frying
4 onions, finely chopped
1/2 cup white wine vinegar
salt and pepper to taste

Michele learned this traditional Venetian sailor's way of marinating sardines from his grandmother. To give it a Valencian touch, mix in a handful of pine nuts and raisins just before serving.

1 Coat the sardines with flour and fry them in a thin layer of hot oil until they are delicately browned on both sides. Drain on paper towels.

2 In a separate pan, slowly fry the onions in oil until they are golden. Remove from the heat, add the vinegar and seasoning, and stir well.

3 Alternate layers of sardines and onions in a deep dish, beginning with sardines and ending with the onions. Cool and refrigerate for at least two hours.

4 To serve, spoon generous portions onto individual plates.

Cheese and quince
Queso con membrillo

for 6 tapas
6 slices of Manchego cheese
3 slices country bread
quince paste

Saltiness and sweetness combine in this traditional Spanish tapa. Michele experiments using different cheeses, including *queso de tetilla*, an obscure, spherical cow's-milk cheese from Galicia. Ultimately, however, nothing can beat the satisfying tanginess of traditional Manchego.

1 Place a piece of Manchego cheese on a half-slice of bread.

2 Place a smaller wedge of quince paste on top of the cheese.

"Valencians stay longer in bars than people elsewhere in Spain. They order a bottle, not a glass, and they sit."

Raquel Sabater Mesón de Labradores, Alicante

If you ask an older resident of Alicante the way to Mesón de Labradores, he might just tell you how, in his rebellious youth, that was where he spent his evenings out. Tapas bars come and go in this port town, which is also a crossroads for tourists on their way to the beaches of the Costa Blanca, but Labradores is a permanent fixture. Now, under the guidance of Raquel Sabater, the founder's granddaughter, it serves up tapas to 300 people nightly in a street once lined with bars and restaurants.

The bar's rustic style was the work of Raquel's grandfather, an antique restorer from Murcia. Copper pans, half-tiled walls, lampshades of dried garlic bulbs, and leather-seated chairs all give a timeless atmosphere that is echoed by the menu. "Most of our recipes are traditional, and hardly vary," says Raquel. "The only one we won't reveal is the chupi-chupi." She licks her fingers to illustrate the meaning of the word. "That's basically a superior open sandwich of good country bread made with beef and a special sauce. My father tasted it in Barcelona, developed the recipe, and it became the house specialty." Although the wind of change has yet to whistle through Labradores, its recipes represent the gastronomic soul of this good-natured corner of Spain.

Spicy pork kabobs
Pinchos morunos

for 4 tapas
3 tbsp. olive oil
2 tbsp. white wine vinegar
¼ tsp. ground cumin
¼ tsp. sweet paprika
¼ tsp. hot paprika
2 tbsp. chopped parsley
2 cloves of garlic, finely chopped
1 lb. 2 oz. lean pork, cut into 1-inch cubes
salt and pepper to taste

4 wooden or metal skewers

Morunos means "Moorish" and, to make an obvious pun, they are certainly "more-ish." Use good-quality pork (a southern Spanish substitute for the Moors' lamb), preferably organic, in order to make tender, richly flavored kabobs. Ideally, cook them on a barbecue, but they taste fine when broiled in an oven.

1 Prepare a marinade by mixing all the ingredients, except for the pork cubes, salt, and pepper.

2 Pour the marinade over the pork cubes and leave for 48 hours.

3 Thread the pork onto the skewers and grill on a high heat for four to five minutes on each side, until all sides are brown. Sprinkle with salt and pepper and serve at once.

Fava bean, ham, and sausage stew
Michirones à la murciana

for 6 tapas
*1 lb. 2 oz. dried fava beans, soaked
for 48 hours
1/4 lb. chorizo or other spicy
sausage, cut into 1/2-inch slices
1/4 lb. serrano ham, thickly cut
and diced
1 ham bone
2 dry red chili peppers, finely chopped
7 cups beef stock
salt to taste*

This is one of the most popular tapas at Labradores. The recipe originated in Murcia, Spain's smallest autonomous region, which lies between Valencia and Andalucía. It is similar to the spicy fava bean and pork stew from Bodega Montaña (*see page 141*), but the beef stock makes this a meatier dish.

1 Place all the ingredients, in the order in which they appear in the ingredients list, in a large saucepan. Pour in just enough stock to cover.

2 Cover the pan and place over a high heat. When the mixture comes to a boil, turn down the heat and cook slowly for one to two hours or until the beans are tender. Top up the stock from time to time, if necessary.

3 Remove the ham bone. Season with salt and pepper (adding salt before this stage would make the beans hard) and serve hot in individual earthenware dishes with chunks of French bread or a few breadsticks.

Poor man's potatoes
Patatas a lo pobre

for 6 tapas

10 tbsp. olive oil, for frying
2 large Spanish onions, sliced into rings
6 medium-sized, firm potatoes,
peeled and sliced
salt to taste
1 tbsp. sherry vinegar
3 cloves of garlic, finely chopped

There are endless variants to this recipe in southern Spain, some of which include red or green peppers. If you want to incorporate peppers, they should be deseeded and sliced and added immediately after the onion and before the potatoes.

1 In a heavy frying pan, heat two tablespoons of oil and fry the onions for 10 minutes, stirring occasionally, until they are golden.

2 Add the remaining oil, allow to heat, then add the potatoes and cook for another 15 to 20 minutes, until they are tender. Season with salt and drain off any excess oil.

3 Mix the vinegar and garlic together, pour over the potatoes, then stir. Serve immediately.

"Most of our recipes are traditional and hardly vary. The only one we won't reveal is the chupi-chupi: a superior open sandwich made with beef and a special sauce. My father tasted it in Barcelona, developed the recipe, and it became the house specialty."

ANDALUCÍA

Manuel Zamora
Casablanca

Rosa María Borja
Isabel Capote Domínguez
La Eslava

Lola García Burgos
Emiliano Sánchez Rincón
Bar Giralda

Julián González Carrasco
Juan Gutiérrez Moreno
Bodegas Campos

Lourdes Ybarra
Bar Europa

Enrique Becerra
Diego Ruiz
Enrique Becerra

No region embodies Moorish Spain as clearly as Andalucía. Other parts of the country may harbor the odd discernible trace of the Moors, but it is in the great arid swath of the south that the 800-year-old Moorish occupation made an unrivaled impact. Architecture, crafts, music, agriculture, fiery eyes, and fiery cuisine are the obvious legacies of a culture that ended in 1492, when the Spanish Catholics captured the Moors' most extraordinary creation: the Alhambra palace, queen of Granada. Looking back at his conquered kingdom, the boy-king Boabdil shed a tear, breathed his "last sigh," and fled into far, and rainfall is rare, even in the winter months, making the problem of drought increasingly severe.

This issue was something the Moors understood well when they set about irrigating huge tracts of land to cultivate a wealth of produce previously unknown to the Iberians. This cultivation is why so many Spanish food words begin with the typically Arabic syllable *al*. Hence, *alcachofa* (artichoke), *alazán* (sorrel), *albahaca* (basil), *albaricoque* (apricot), *alcaparra* (caper), *almendra* (almond), and *almíbar* (syrup).

The Moorish occupiers also added layers to the previous Roman and

"Olive trees march over the horizon, and almond trees explode into frothy pink and white blossoms. Fighting bulls graze in the Guadalquivír Valley, oranges dangle from foliage in town centers, goats trip up rocky hillsides, tuna is netted off Cádiz."

exile. The mountain pass he followed still bears this epithet, as does so much else in Andalucía that is connected to the Moors. If you have a "last tapa," make it here.

Lunar landscapes of karst and shale roll into the heat haze, olive trees march over the horizon, and almond trees explode into frothy pink and white blossoms. Fighting bulls graze in the Guadalquivír Valley, oranges dangle from foliage in town centers, goats trip up rocky hillsides, tuna is netted off Cádiz. In the southeast, vast fields of *plásticas* (plastic greenhouses) force-grow much of Europe's supply of avocados, artichokes, tomatoes, and green beans on a year-round basis. The region's temperatures never descend Iberian palate with their vast orange and lemon groves, chilled gazpacho (vegetable soup), dates, and sugarcane. Thus the sweet tooth hit town, and it is still evident in the numerous dishes and delicacies that include honey or dried fruits. It is said that tapas originated in Seville and, whether or not this is true, the city's inhabitants are certainly masters of the art.

Hedonistic, rococo, and extrovert, Seville possesses little of the poetic earnestness that filters through the arches of Córdoba's Mezquita or Granada's noble setting. Seville is a composite of stage sets, each a tiny plaza that, more often than not, is flanked by a saffron-colored church, orange trees, and a couple of tapas bars for easy exits to the wings.

The *sevillianos'* sense of drama peaks during *Semana Santa* (Easter week) and *Feria* (April fair), when women strut in the flounces of flamenco dresses or in severe riding suits and gaucho hats, while men in penitents' hoods carry statues of Christ, or clad in riding gear, direct their mounts with macho panache to the nearest source of *fino*.

Throughout the year, popular tapas bars in Seville see people spilling out onto the pavement, squeezing up on a corner ledge or a sherry-barrel, or kicking the sawdust next to a bunch of matadors in order to wolf down an ever-varied tapas lunch. You could almost set your watch by these social gatherings, so entrenched are they in daily life.

The classic Sevillian drink comes from nearby Jerez de la Frontera. The origins of sherry have their roots, as do all Spanish wines, with the Phoenicians, but sherry, a fortified wine, was developed over the centuries as a way of avoiding spoilage. It became popular in England during the sixteenth century, after Sir Francis Drake seized nearly 3,000 barrels of it from the Spanish Armada in 1587. Well-to-do Londoners in particular developed a taste for the stolen wine, and this was the genesis of a flourishing industry that left many English merchants' names attached to numerous bodegas, or wineries.

Whether it is a refreshing, tongue-searingly dry fino, a honey-colored *amontillado*, a rich, golden *oloroso*, or a syrupy *dulce*, sherry's incarnations suit every palate and tapa—despite the local preference for *manzanilla*, a slightly saltier version of fino that is produced in the seaside town of Sanlúcar de Barrameda. When not consuming sherry chilled, Andalucíans use it in vinegar form as a piquant addition to gazpachos and vegetable-based tapas.

Bullfighting plays a fanatical role in Andalucía's multiple fiestas, making *rabo de toro* (oxtail) an entrenched favorite on the region's tapas menus (although the recent threat of bovine diseases has put the brakes on this particular taste). Fresh seafood is a permanent feature, too, whether in the myriad of tapas bars found along the coast or in the heart of inland Andalucía.

Stand on a bridge crossing the Guadalquivír River in Seville, fifty-six miles from the estuary, and you can sniff the salt in the air, just like Ferdinand Magellan, Juan Sebastián Elcano, and Christopher Columbus, all of whom set sail from here during Spain's preoccupation with the high seas. New World plunder brought back in their ships' holds financed the city's wealth of monuments, peaking in the seventeenth century with the baroque style and reflected in the great Sevillian school of painting by Pacheco, Velàzquez, and Murillo.

Other New World booty took the more prosaic form of potatoes, tomatoes, corn, cocoa, custard apples—and, of course, tobacco. Seville's old tobacco factory, situated right next to the harbor, contains the shadow of the legendary Carmen, stamping her feet and howling for love. The pungent whiff of cigar smoke permeates many a tapas bar, while the food imported from the Americas has produced yet another sea of change in Andalucían cuisine.

It's hard not to feel it. Andalucía is all about passion and tragedy, emotions, extremes, strong flavors, hot sun, and cool soups. Cook the tapas of this magnetic region and you'll be propelled into an extraordinary world. Just make sure the flamenco music is loud enough.

Manuel Zamora   Casablanca, Seville

Casablanca is another of Andalucía's hidden secrets, tucked down a side street in central Seville behind a nondescript closed door. Push it open and you enter a tiny gastronomic heaven frequented by Seville's top brass and the odd bullfighter. The chef, a generous, ebullient Andalucían in his early forties, Manuel Zamora thinks, breathes, and probably dreams food. "I started as a dishwasher in a five-star restaurant at the age of fifteen and never stopped asking the cooks and staff questions about what was being made," he says. He kept this questioning attitude as he worked his way up the ladder, via Las Palmas, to the Parador de Carmona before entering the highly rated Casablanca. Having cooked tapas, lunches, and dinners six days a week, Manuel will spend his day off tending the olive trees, tomatoes, and doves in his garden or looking at cookbooks.

Intuitive in his approach, Manuel is also sensitive to his customers' tastes. "I'm inspired by what I see in the market," he says, "And ninety percent of what I use is Andalucían. Even the foie gras is local and the demi-glaze is typically Spanish. There's no menu here and every dish we make must be excellent." The one permanent fixture is seasoned mashed potatoes, served with your first drink (free) and much imitated but never equaled by other tapas bars.

Seasoned mashed potatoes
Patatas aliñadas

for 6 tapas

2 lb. 4 oz. new potatoes, scrubbed
3 spring onions, white part only,
finely chopped
3 green peppers, finely chopped
1/2 cup plus 2 tbsp. extra-virgin olive oil
3 tbsp. white wine vinegar
salt and pepper

Casablanca's hallmark tapa is generously bathed in extra-virgin olive oil from Baena, rated as Andalucía's premier oil. Don't worry if you can't find it, but use the best substitute you can find. In typical Manuel fashion, this is a delicious tapa created from the simplest ingredients.

1 Cook the potatoes in boiling, salted water for about 20 minutes or until they are tender.

2 Remove the skins and mash the potatoes, then push the mashed potatoes through a sieve or potato ricer. Add the onions and peppers.

3 Slowly add the oil and vinegar, beating until the potatoes are thick and creamy. If more oil and vinegar is necessary, add in proportions of three parts oil to one part vinegar.

4 Season with salt and pepper and serve immediately on small plates.

Seafood pasta
Fideos à la marinera

for 6 tapas

1 medium onion, diced
2 medium green peppers, diced
2 tomatoes, diced
2 cloves of garlic, minced
olive oil, for frying
about 1/3 cup white wine
4 1/2 cups water
1/4 tsp. saffron threads, infused in boiling water
1/2 lb. clams, well-scrubbed; discard any that will not close
6 oz. cuttlefish, cleaned and cut into small strips
6 oz. shrimp, peeled
4 oz. hake or cod, filleted and cut into small pieces
salt and pepper to taste
8 oz. short lengths of spaghetti or a pasta shape such as tubetti lunghi

Although tricky to prepare, this tapa looks and tastes so terrific that you may want to increase the quantities to make it into a main dish. If you can't find vermicelli, substitute fine spaghetti, chopped into manageable lengths.

1 In a casserole or heavy-bottomed sauté pan, fry the onion, peppers, tomatoes, and garlic in the olive oil until soft.

2 Add the white wine and cook for about 10 minutes to reduce the liquid.

3 Add the water and saffron liquid and cook over a high heat for 15 minutes.

4 Add the clams, cuttlefish, shrimp, hake, seasoning, and pasta noodles and continue to cook over a low heat for about 10 minutes, until the fish and pasta are tender and the liquid has been absorbed. Discard any clams that have not opened. Serve in individual earthenware dishes.

Tortilla de patatas
Potato tortilla

for 6 tapas
1/2 cup olive oil
2 lb. 4 oz. potatoes, peeled and cubed
3 eggs, beaten
salt and pepper to taste

Manuel serves this classic Spanish tortilla, made typically with potatoes, with an ambrosial sauce based on whiskey (*see below*)

1 Heat the olive oil in a deep frying pan. Cook the potatoes in the oil over a very low heat for about 15 minutes, until they are tender but not brown.

2 In a bowl, mix the potatoes with the beaten eggs, and season to taste. Pour the mixture back into the frying pan and cook over a low heat for three to four minutes. When the tortilla is firm but not dry, cover the frying pan with a plate of equal size and, grasping the plate and pan, flip the tortilla out onto the plate.

3 Carefully slide the tortilla back into the pan and cook for another three minutes to brown the other side.

4 Turn out onto a serving plate and cool for at least five minutes. Slices can be served hot or at room temperature, covered with whiskey sauce (*see below*).

"I'm inspired by what I see in the market. Ninety percent of what I use is Andalucían. Even the foie gras is local and the demi-glaze I use is typically Spanish."

Whiskey sauce
Salsa de whiskey

for 6 tapas
3 cloves of garlic, finely sliced
2 tbsp. olive oil
1 tbsp. butter
1 tbsp. lemon juice
1 tbsp. whiskey
1 tbsp. strong beef stock

Manuel serves this sauce as an accompaniment for the above tortilla. It's a combination that may sound odd, but given Andalucían enthusiasm for high spirits, it is hardly surprising! This sauce also tastes good with meats such as beef.

1 Sauté the garlic slices in the olive oil until they are tender.

2 Add the butter, lemon juice, whiskey, and beef stock. Cook over a low heat, stirring occasionally, for 15 minutes or until reduced.

Chicken legs with prunes and nuts in blackberry sauce
Pularda rellena de frutos secos en salsa de zarza mora

for 12 tapas
2/3 cup pine nuts
about 1/3 cup chopped walnuts
about 1/3 cup unsalted pistachio
nuts, shelled and chopped
5 oz. pitted prunes, chopped
12 organic, boneless chicken legs
salt and pepper to taste
2 tbsp. olive oil
1/2 lb. garlic cloves
2 potatoes, cut into 1/8-inch slices
2 small onions, sliced into half-moons
1 cup sweet Málaga wine

for the blackberry sauce
5 oz. fresh or frozen blackberries
1/2 cup granulated sugar
2 tbsp. balsamic vinegar

Moorish influences rule in this luscious concoction of prunes, nuts, fruit, chicken, and sweet wine. Remember that you can substitute any dark dessert wine for the Málaga variety.

1 Mix the nuts and prunes together, then stuff the chicken legs with the mixture. Tie each leg together with kitchen string.

2 Place the stuffed legs on baking sheets, season, drizzle with olive oil, surround with garlic cloves, onions, and potatoes, and bake in an oven preheated to 400°F for 30 to 35 minutes, until the chicken is cooked.

3 To make the sauce, heat the berries and sugar with a few tablespoons of water, stirring to dissolve the sugar in the berry juices. Add the vinegar, bring to a boil, then cook until syrupy; it will thicken more as it cools. Set aside.

4 Gently warm the wine over a low heat. Transfer the chicken legs, garlic, and onions to a platter, pour on the wine, and flambé immediately by touching the edge of the platter with the flame of a match. Serve the chicken accompanied by the sauce.

Andalucían-style spinach with chickpeas
Espinacas con garbanzos à la andaluza

for 6 tapas
2 lb. 4 oz. fresh spinach, washed
and destalked
1/4 cup olive oil
10 oz. cooked chickpeas
1 tsp. ground cumin
salt and pepper to taste
3 cloves of garlic
1 slice of bread, fried in oil until golden
1 tsp. red wine vinegar
2 tbsp. water
1 1/2 tsp. paprika

This classic Andalucían dish has traveled to tapas bars all over Spain, such is its earthy appeal. The spinach and chickpeas are, surprisingly, Moorish imports.

1 In a covered saucepan, cook the spinach, using only the water that clings to it after washing, for about four minutes, until it is wilted. Cool, then press out the excess water. Chop roughly.

2 Sauté the spinach in the oil over a low heat for about one minute. Add the chickpeas, cumin, salt, and pepper, and stir thoroughly.

3 Pound the garlic and fried bread with a mortar and pestle or chop them in a blender until fine. Add to the spinach and mix well.

4 Add the vinegar, water, and paprika, and cook over a low heat, stirring constantly, for about one minute. Serve at once in individual earthenware dishes.

Rosa María Borja
Isabel Capote Domínguez La Eslava, Seville

You could easily miss out on La Eslava, for it is tucked down a backstreet off the vast Alameda de Hércules. Yet this hip haunt is quintessentially Sevillian, netting an eclectic range of customers, from local artists and intellectuals to those in the know from further afield. Behind the bar, energetic owner Sixto Tovar Gutierrez juggles phone calls with tapas or beers, while in the kitchen his French wife, Rosa María Bórja, accomplishes La Eslava's miracles in tandem with Isabel Capote Dominguez. According to Isabel, "Together with vegetables, olive oil is the most important characteristic of Andalucían cuisine." Describing the approach of this glamorous duet, she says, "When we make a dish, we look at the colors and flavors, but if it doesn't taste right we abandon it."

Rosa María appreciates suggestions from her customers. "Our customers propose ideas, which we follow up," she says. "They adore soups, as they take a long time to prepare at home." Ask her to compare Andalucía with her native southwest France and Rosa María says, "French food is, of course, very good, but Andalucía's basic produce has far more flavor. The gazpacho my mother made in Toulouse was never as good as the gazpacho they make here." Even better is La Eslava's renowned salmorejo, often imitated but never surpassed.

Spinach and shrimp loaf
Pudin de espinacas

for 4 tapas
14 oz. spinach, washed and destalked
1 medium onion, finely chopped
2 medium tomatoes, finely chopped
2 tbsp. olive oil
1/4 lb. raw shrimp, peeled
salt and pepper to taste
1/2 cup milk
1/2 cup heavy cream
4 eggs

This cold, mousse-like tapa is ideal for hot weather, when appetites are not too big. La Eslava's customers favor beer or sangría as their summer drinks, and this tapa makes the perfect accompaniment for either.

1 In a covered saucepan, cook the spinach, using only the water that clings to the leaves after washing, over a medium heat for about four minutes. Drain, and wring out the excess water by pressing the cooked leaves between two dinner plates; the spinach must be very dry. Set aside.

2 Sauté the onion and tomatoes in the olive oil until tender. Turn up the heat and allow some of the liquid to evaporate. Add the spinach and shrimp, season, and stir. Cook over a low heat for three to four minutes, then cool.

3 Put the shrimp and spinach mixture into a blender and add the milk, cream, and eggs. Blend until smooth and creamy. Season to taste.

4 Pour into a lightly oiled loaf pan. Place the loaf pan into a roasting pan filled with two to three inches of water. Bake at 350ºF for about 45 minutes, until firm (a skewer inserted into the center should come out clean). Cool, then refrigerate for at least two hours.

5 To serve, turn out of the pan and cut into slices of the desired thickness.

Chilled tomato and garlic soup
Salmorejo

for 4 tapas
1 lb. 2 oz. ripe tomatoes
1/2 lb. day-old bread, torn into pieces
1 cup olive oil
1 tbsp. sherry vinegar
1 clove of garlic
salt and pepper to taste
1 hard-boiled egg, chopped (optional)
2 oz. serrano ham or prosciutto, chopped (optional)

Although *salmorejo* originated in Córdoba, neighboring Seville has taken to it with a passion. It is basically a thicker, creamier version of gazpacho, and works equally well as a soup or dip. The most important element, the tomatoes, must be plump and juicy or the soup will lack its raison d'être.

1 Combine the tomatoes and bread in a blender and mix well. Add the oil, vinegar, garlic, salt, and pepper, and blend until smooth and thick.

2 Serve as a dip with chunks of French bread, or as a soup, drizzled with extra-virgin olive oil. Add a sprinkling of diced serrano ham and chopped hard-boiled egg, if desired.

Potato and cod stew
Purrusalda

for 4 tapas
8 oz. salt cod
4 leeks, cleaned and coarsely chopped
4 tbsp. olive oil
2 lb. 4 oz. potatoes, peeled and diced
11 cups fish stock
3 ripe tomatoes, chopped
salt and pepper to taste

The classic marriage of cod and potatoes has been developed by Rosa María and Isabel into a hearty, appetizing tapa, lifted by tomatoes and olive oil.

1 Soak the salt cod in water for 48 hours, changing the water twice a day. Rinse. Flake the flesh, leaving any bones and the skin behind.

2 In a large saucepan or stockpot, sauté the leeks in the oil until tender. Add the potatoes, then sauté over a very low heat for 15 more minutes.

3 Add the fish stock and tomatoes, bring to a boil, and simmer for 20 minutes.

4 Add the flaked salt cod and simmer for 10 minutes. Season to taste and serve hot in individual soup bowls.

"French food is, of course, very good, but Andalucía's basic produce has more flavor. The gazpacho made in Toulouse was never as good as the gazpacho they make here."

Honey-baked chicken thighs
Muslos de pollo à la miel

for 4 tapas
1 cup honey
about 1/2 cup butter
1 tsp. curry powder
1 1/2 tsp. dry mustard
about 1/3 cup ketchup
8 chicken thighs

This simple recipe offers some interesting flavor contrasts, all dominated by the sweetness of the honey—yet another Moorish legacy. It makes an excellent tapa to accompany dry white wine or dry sherry on a summer's day.

1 To prepare the honey sauce, combine all the ingredients, except the chicken thighs, in a saucepan. Mix well and bring to a boil. Remove from the heat.

2 Place the chicken thighs in a roasting pan, pour on the sauce, and bake in a preheated oven at 350°F for about 35 minutes or until the chicken is dark, glossy, and fully cooked. Serve hot.

Lola García Burgos
Emiliano Sánchez Rincón   Bar Giralda, Seville

Just behind Seville's emblematic Giralda, a towering twelfth-century minaret
topped by a Renaissance belfry, lies a bar with the same name, converted in 1934
from Arab baths into one of Seville's most architecturally stunning watering holes.
Run by Francisco Sánchez González, its tiled walls, vaulted ceilings, stuccoed
arches, and marble-topped tables create a classic meeting place for Sevillian
society. Because it is open from breakfast until the early hours, Bar Giralda
functions more like a Parisian grand café than a traditional tapas bar.

Sevillians gather here not only for the elegant setting, but also for the
constantly changing tapas menu. This is the work of Francisco's wife, Lola Gracía
Burgos, and chef Emiliano Sánchez Pincón, a Sevillian by birth, who has perfected
his art in Bar Giralda's kitchen during the last nineteen years.

"I started working here when I was seventeen and learned everything I know
from the other cooks," Emiliano says. "The tapas are now a collaboration between
Lola and me. We're always experimenting and varying the list." On the blackboard
is scrawled the tapa of the day, generally based on meat or fish, as well as the rest
of the menu. "Seville represents the heart of Andalucían traditions, so we try to
reflect that," he continues. "Málaga, for example, concentrates mainly on seafood,
but the ingredients that are eternal are onions, tomatoes, and red peppers; I couldn't
do without them." And few Sevillians could do without this retreat.

Potatoes of great importance
Patatas à la importancia

for 4 tapas

*2 large potatoes, peeled and cut into
1/2-inch slices*
1/4 lb. cooked ham, in thin slices
*1/4 lb. French Chaumes or Port
Salut cheese, cut into thin slices*
salt to taste
beaten egg, for coating
all-purpose flour, for coating
1 cup olive oil, for frying

for the sauce
2 tbsp. olive oil
7 cloves of garlic, thinly sliced
1 bunch of Italian parsley, chopped
2 tbsp. all-purpose flour
1 cup white wine

This is another example of Spain's sustaining peasant snacks, made from basic ingredients with strong flavors.

1 Between two potato slices, place one slice of ham and one slice of cheese. Season with salt. Dip in the beaten egg, then in the flour, and fry in hot oil until the potato is golden and fully cooked. Remove.

2 To make the sauce, heat the oil in a frying pan. Add the garlic and sauté until tender. Add the parsley and stir.

Blend in the flour, stirring until the mixture has thickened. Take the pan off the heat and stir constantly, adding

3 When the wine has been added, put the pan back on the heat and bring to a boil, stirring. Simmer for five minutes. Pour the sauce over the potatoes and serve immediately.

Roast chicken breasts stuffed with salmon
Pechugas de pollo rellenas de salmón con salsa de curry

for 4 tapas
2 chicken breast fillets
olive oil
6 oz. sliced smoked salmon
pepper to taste
1/2 cup plus 2 tbsp. curry sauce
(see below)

This simple but effective tapa can be prepared in advance and heated at the last minute. Organic chicken is best, since it tends to have more flavor and stands up to the strong tastes of the salmon and curry sauce.

1 Place the chicken breasts on a rack in a shallow pan and brush with olive oil. Season and roast in an oven preheated to 300°F for about 25 minutes. The chicken should be almost cooked; check by cutting into the breast with a sharp knife. Cool slightly. Reduce the oven to 250°F.

2 Slice each breast in half lengthwise, without cutting through, and open. Stuff with several slices of salmon and season with pepper. Wrap in aluminum foil and place in a shallow baking tray. Return to the oven for 20 minutes or until the chicken is fully cooked.

3 Remove the chicken from the foil. Cut each breast crosswise into four slices, arrange on a platter, and pour the curry sauce over the top. Serve immediately.

Curry sauce
Salsa de curry

for 4 tapas
1/2 large onion
1 tsp. curry powder
1/2 cup mayonnaise

This sauce is ideal served with the salmon-stuffed chicken breasts (*above*), or served with bread as a spicy dip.

1 Remove the outer layer of the onion. Parboil the rest of the onion, drain, cool, and finely chop.

2 Combine all the ingredients in a blender and mix well.

Julián González Carrasco
Juan Gutiérrez Moreno   Bodegas Campos, Córdoba

The sober frontage of Córdoba's most successful restaurant spells out its attitude to food: quality and finesse. This is what attracts the town's movers and shakers to dine here in studied calm. Between the rooms of this labyrinthine restaurant lie typically Córdoban patios, thick with perfumes and bright with geraniums; shady corridors lined with sherry barrels; and tiled floors clicking with the heels of fame.

More than anywhere else, Bodegas Campos provides a journey into the heart of Andalucía. Since it opened in 1908, the restaurant has fed a stream of celebrities, including the Duchess of Alba, Paco Peña, and Tony Blair. Yet despite its success, it maintains a personal approach, dealt out by four chefs and twenty cooks and headed by Julián González Carasco and Juan Gutierrez Moreno. For Juan, "Andalucían cuisine is the best, after French, which is the basis of everything. Our advantage lies in the quality of our products: the fresh fish, vegetables, and excellent oils and vinegars." Quality in all respects is the basis of the exquisite tapas which, although simple to prepare, keep rulers, matadors, and divas coming back for more.

Chilled tomato soup with aged sherry vinegar
Gazpacho de tomate con vinagre de Pedro Ximénez

for 4 tapas

2 lb. 4 oz. plump, vine-ripened tomatoes, chopped

1 lb. 2 oz. fresh breadcrumbs, made from a crusty loaf

³/₄ cup Pedro Ximénez vinegar or similar mature sherry vinegar

2¹/₄ cups extra-virgin olive oil

salt and pepper to taste

This is one of many gazpacho recipes: a more liquid soup than salmorejo, but similarly dependent on juicy, flavor-packed tomatoes. A dish with this much sherry vinegar is something of an acquired taste, so start with a quarter of the quantity given and add the rest to taste. This gazpacho can be served with little side dishes of diced ham, green pepper, cucumber, and tomatoes to sprinkle on top. More like a superior, seasoned tomato juice, it makes the ultimate refreshing summer tapa.

1 Put all the ingredients into a blender and then blend to a smooth, thick, but juicy consistency.

2 Adjust the seasoning to taste, then refrigerate for at least two hours. Serve cold in glasses with a drizzle of olive oil.

Country-style potatoes with chorizo and peppers
Patatas cortijeras con picadillo de chorizo

for 4 tapas

14 oz. potatoes, peeled and thinly sliced
¹/₄ cup butter
¹/₄ cup olive oil for frying
4 oz. onion, thinly sliced
1 oz. red pepper, thinly sliced
1 oz. green pepper, thinly sliced
3 cloves of garlic, thinly sliced
1 oz. serrano ham or prosciutto, cut into thin strips
2 oz. chorizo or similar spicy sausage, cut into ¹/₂-inch slices and lightly fried
2 eggs
salt and pepper to taste

Developed in the kitchen by Julián and Juan, this recipe exploits the abundant fresh local vegetables, with the chorizo and ham acting as little more than seasoning. It's a perfect, sustaining combination enveloped by lightly cooked egg.

1 Fry the potatoes in the butter and two tablespoons of the oil over a very low heat for about 25 minutes, until tender. Remove, leaving the fat behind, and put them in a large bowl. Set aside.

2 In the same pan, sauté the onion and peppers, adding more oil if needed. When these are tender, add the garlic and cook until golden. Add the vegetables to the potatoes, stir in the meats, and set aside.

3 Fry the eggs in a little oil until the white is firm. Add them to the vegetable and meat mixture and stir to break up the eggs. Combine all the ingredients, season, and tip onto a serving platter.

Fried pork loin and ham balls
Bolitas de flamenquín

for 6 tapas
8 oz. pork loin, cut into thin strips
juice of 1 lemon
4 oz. Iberian or serrano ham
(or prosciutto)
salt and pepper to taste
2 tbsp. all-purpose flour
2 eggs, beaten
1/2 cup dried breadcrumbs
olive oil, for frying

Quite simply delicious, this is an excellent tapa for large numbers of people, as the meatballs can be prepared in advance and served cold. The zing of the lemon juice makes all the difference.

1 Marinate the pork loin in the lemon juice for one hour.

2 Place a piece of ham on each pork strip, season, and roll up lengthwise to form cylinders.

3 Cut each cylinder into one-inch pieces, and shape these into balls.

4 Dip the balls in the flour, then the egg, then the breadcrumbs, and fry a few at a time in very hot oil, browning on all sides. Drain on paper towels and serve promptly.

"Andalucían cuisine is the best, after French, which is the basis of everything. Our advantage lies in the quality of our products: the fresh fish, vegetables, and excellent oils and vinegars."

Fritata of garden vegetables
Fritura de la huerta

for 4 tapas
2 oz. onion, cut into thin rings
2 tbsp. flour
2 oz. cauliflower, separated into florets and briefly cooked
1 egg, beaten
1/2 cup dried breadcrumbs
2 oz. eggplant, peeled and cut into small cubes
1 tbsp. milk
olive oil, for frying
salt to taste

The choice of vegetables is yours but, as always, follow the seasons for the best results. Obvious alternatives to those used in this recipe are green and red peppers. The light batter produces a crisp coating that resembles tempura.

1 Dip the onion rings in flour. Dip the cauliflower first in the flour, then in the egg, then in the breadcrumbs. Moisten the eggplant cubes in milk and then coat with flour.

2 Heat about 21/2 inches of olive oil in a frying pan and, when hot, cook the vegetables separately. Drain on paper towels and then add salt to taste.

3 Arrange attractively on a plate and serve promptly with a salmorejo dip (*see page 168*).

Lourdes Ybarra Bar Europa, Seville

*In the last year of the twentieth century, Bar Europa underwent a major facelift under
the guidance of its new owner, Neus Bragat, from Barcelona. Before her aegis, this was
a neglected, family-owned bar whose cuisine was limited to tripe stew. By restoring
the premises to its original 1920s splendor, Neus put this classic Sevillian tapas bar
back on the map and at the same time injected northern elements into the menu. It is
now one of the few places in Seville to serve cava, and the changing tapas menu
sometimes features white or black* butifarra *(blood sausage) or similar Catalan
specialties. The menu aside, Bar Europa embodies a typically elegant Sevillian setting.*

*Easily visible through the kitchen hatch behind the long, wooden bar is the chef,
Lourdes Ybarra, a native of a nearby village, where she ran her own bar before coming
to the big city. "Most of my ideas and methods come either from cooking school or
from my grandmother," she says. "I had seven brothers and sisters, and, although I was
the youngest, I ended up doing all the cooking. It's simply something I love doing!"
Something to bear in mind when preparing any of her tapas.*

Chilled almond soup
Ajo blanco

for 4 tapas

8 oz. blanched almonds
3 cloves of garlic
about 1½ cups fresh white breadcrumbs
2¼ cups water
2 tbsp. sherry vinegar
salt to taste
6 tbsp. olive oil
8 muscatel (or similar) grapes
extra-virgin olive oil, to serve

This soup, invented by the Moors to counteract Andalucía's scorching-hot summers, can look divinely minimalist served in white bowls and garnished with floating white muscatel grapes. It makes a refreshing change from some of Andalucía's stronger flavors, as the almond flavor is extremely subtle.

1 Finely grind the almonds and garlic in a blender. Add the breadcrumbs, water, vinegar, and salt, and blend for two minutes.

2 Slowly add the olive oil, while continuing to blend, until you have a creamy liquid. Refrigerate for at least one hour.

3 Serve in individual soup bowls, with a grape or two and a light drizzle of extra-virgin olive oil in each one.

Salt cod and orange salad
Ensalada de bacalao con naranja

for 4 tapas
1 lb. 12 oz. salt cod
11 oz. juicy orange segments, skin and seeds removed, diced
2 tbsp. chives, snipped
4 black olives
extra-virgin olive oil to taste

This ultrasimple tapa offers a refreshing combination of flavors, but it is essential to use good-quality salt cod and luscious oranges. If you have individual molds, so much the better, as cutting slices of this dish tends to make it crumble.

1 Soak the salt cod in water for 48 hours, changing the water twice a day. Remove the flesh and flake, discarding the skin and bones.

2 Mix the orange flesh with the chives, then divide the mixture into individual molds. Top with the flaked salt cod and compress well.

3 Refrigerate for at least one hour before turning upside down onto plates to serve.

4 Decorate with a black olive and drizzle with olive oil.

Ratatouille with quail eggs
Pisto con huevo de codorniz

for 4 tapas
6 green peppers, diced
1 large onion, diced
olive oil
1 lb. 2 oz. eggplant, peeled and diced
1 lb. 2 oz. zucchini, diced
1 lb. 2 oz. tomatoes, diced
salt and pepper to taste
4 quail eggs

Pisto originated in La Mancha, but soon conquered the south and became Andalucía's answer to Provençal ratatouille: a mixture of braised Mediterranean vegetables served with a fried egg. When preparing the vegetables, keep them in separate dishes so that you can easily add them successively.

1 In a large pan, sauté the peppers and onion in olive oil until tender. Add the eggplant and sauté for five more minutes. Add the zucchini and sauté for three more minutes.

2 Add the tomatoes, lower the heat, and simmer for 20 minutes. Season five minutes before the cooking time has ended.

3 Quickly fry the quail eggs in some olive oil.

4 To serve, heap generous portions of ratatouille on individual serving plates and top with a fried egg.

Enrique Becerra
Diego Ruiz
Enrique Becerra, Seville

This humming tapas bar, within one of Seville's most successful restaurants, was opened in 1979 by Enrique Becerra, a sevilliano with five generations of bar-restaurants pumping through his blood. The tapas menu changes daily, the result of a collaboration between Enrique and his head chef, Diego Ruiz. Madrid-born and trained, Diego started working in restaurants at the age of fifteen, remaining in the capital until he took over the ovens at Enrique Becerra three years ago. "The basic produce here, such as vegetables, chickpeas, lentils, and chorizo, is excellent," he says. "In the north, they go for more sophisticated foods such as baby eel, caviar, or smoked salmon, but you can do fantastic things with simple, good-quality ingredients. Here, there's a taste for earthy, primitive dishes."

Diego has no delusions about the demands of his profession. "It requires long hours and total dedication," he says, "But cooking is about inspiration—like any art form. The main thing is to like what you're doing." So perch on a bar stool, order a manzanilla, munch on Becerra's succulent olives ladled from an earthenware pot, and you'll soon be humming a few bars from Carmen.

Asparagus and shrimp tarts
Pudin de espárragos verdes y gambas

for 4 tapas

1/2 medium onion, finely chopped
olive oil
4 oz. shrimp, peeled and chopped
4 oz. green asparagus, preferably wild, cut into small pieces
1/4 cup dry sherry
1 cup whipping cream
3 eggs, beaten
salt and white pepper to taste
mayonnaise, to serve

The Spanish word *pudin*, an aborted version of the English "pudding," is used to describe a savory tapa that resembles a French mousse. This version has a pleasingly rough texture and undemanding flavors.

1 A day before serving, sauté the onion in a little olive oil until soft. Add the shrimp, asparagus, and sherry, and cook over a low heat until the liquid has almost disappeared.

2 Add the cream, eggs, and a little salt and pepper, and mix well.

3 Pour into lightly oiled, individual tart pans. Set these into a roasting or cake pan filled with about a half-inch of water and bake in a 350°F oven for 35 minutes. Remove from the oven, cool, and then refrigerate for 12 hours.

4 Just before serving, turn out the tarts, place on individual plates, and top each with a spoonful of mayonnaise.

Lentil and chorizo stew
Lentejas estofadas

for 4 tapas

*8 oz. green or brown lentils,
soaked overnight*
about 1/3 cup virgin olive oil
1 1/2 tsp. paprika
1 small green pepper, diced
1 small onion, diced
1 small, ripe tomato, peeled and diced
1 bay leaf
3 cloves of garlic
*4 oz. chorizo or other spicy
sausage, sliced*
4 oz. blood sausage, sliced
1 small carrot, peeled and sliced
8 oz. potatoes, peeled and diced

Well-blended, earthy flavors are the characteristics of this classic tapa, simply prepared according to Diego's tastes.

1 Combine all the ingredients, except the potatoes, in a heavy saucepan. Cover with cold water and bring to a boil. Reduce the heat and simmer for about 20 minutes.

2 Add the potatoes and continue to simmer for about 10 more minutes, until the potatoes and lentils are tender. Serve hot in individual earthenware dishes.

Minted lamb meatballs
Albóndigas de cordero à la hierbabuena

for 6 tapas

*1 lb. 2 oz. lamb, ground or finely
chopped*
salt and pepper to taste
3 cloves of garlic, finely chopped
1 tbsp. chopped, fresh mint
2 small eggs, beaten
4 tbsp. soft breadcrumbs
1/2 cup dry sherry
1 tbsp. olive oil, for sautéing

For the sauce

2 onions, finely chopped
1 clove garlic, finely chopped
1 tbsp. olive oil, for sautéing
1 cup thick tomato paste
1 tbsp. dry sherry
water, for thinning

Although Spain offers numerous variants on the meatball theme, these are arguably some of the tastiest in the entire country!

1 Combine all the meatball ingredients, except the olive oil, in a large bowl and mix well. Form the meat into one-inch balls and sauté in oil until lightly browned on all sides. Drain on paper towels and set aside.

2 In the same pan, sauté the onions and garlic for the sauce in olive oil until soft. Add the tomato paste and sherry and simmer for 10 minutes. Remove from the heat.

3 In a blender, puree the sauce until smooth, adding a little water if it's too thick. Return the sauce to the sauté pan and add the meatballs. Bring to a boil and cook over a medium heat for about 10 minutes. Serve hot.

RECOMMENDED TAPAS BARS

* Bars featured in this book

THE BASQUE COUNTRY

Aloña Berri Bar, Calle Bermingham 24, Gros, San Sebastián Tel: (943) 290818

A mouthful of hot foie gras with fig or a tasty bite of crab or langoustine are among the offerings at one of San Sebastián's most sophisticated tapas bars.

Casa Bartolo, Calle Fermin Calbeton 38, San Sebastián Tel: (943) 421743

Mean classics of Basque cuisine are served in tapas portions at the bar. Bacalao pil-pil (salt cod cooked with olive oil and garlic), bacalao à la vizcaina (salt cod in a tomato, onion, and pepper sauce) and bacalao en cebollado (salt cod with onions) are the stars.

*Baserri, Calle San Nicolas, 32, 31001 Pamplona Tel: (948) 222021
www.restaurantebaserri.com

In a street that is wall-to-wall tapas bars with a bacalao shop thrown in for good measure, this is the ultimate destination for top-class food.

*Bar Bergara, Calle General Artetxe 8, Gros, San Sebastián Tel: (943) 275026

Pintxos faithfuls flock to this prizewinning temple of delicacies in San Sebastián's art-deco quarter. Whether warm or cold, each dish is a work of art.

*La Cuchara de San Telmo, Calle 31 de Agosto 28, San Sebastián Tel: (943) 420840

Revel in imaginative concoctions of miniature gourmet cuisine if you can squeeze your way into the bar. Outside on the terrace, relax in the shadow of the old church of San Telmo.

Bar Fitero, Calle Estafeta 58, Pamplona Tel: (948) 222006

A third generation works hard to keep the tapas quality intact, from the roquefort crêpes to the spinach croquettes.

Ganbara, Calle San Jeronimo 21, San Sebastián Tel: (943) 422575

A feast for the eyes and the gastronomic imagination, this is one of the old quarter's most popular pintxos bars.

Kursaal, Avenida de la Zurriola 1, Gros, San Sebastián Tel: (943) 003162

Sophisticated tapas are served in this seaside cafeteria located inside Rafael Moneo's magnificent Kursaal.

*Bar Txepetxa, Calle Pescaderia 5, San Sebastián Tel: (943) 422227

Manuel's family bar has been winning pintxos prizes for more than a decade. The marinated anchovies are hard to beat.

CATALONIA

Casa Alfonso, Roger de Lluria 6, Barcelona Tel: (93) 301 9783

1930s Barcelona on the edge of Eixample offers quality Iberian meat tapas and luscious tortillas to famished lady shoppers.

*Cal Pep, Plaça de les Olles 8, Barcelona Tel: (93) 310 7961

A landmark bar where exquisite seafood tapas are served in sociable mayhem.

Can Paixano, Carrer Reina Cristina 7, Barcelona Tel: (93) 310 0839

Hidden in a grid of waterside streets, one of Barcelona's most atmospheric bars attracts cava-quaffing harbor-workers.

*Comerç24, Carrer Comerç 24, Barcelona Tel: (93) 319 2102

The ultimate designer venue for the ultimate designer tapas signed by Carlos Abellan.

Convent dels Angels, Plaça dels Angels 5-6, Barcelona Tel: (93) 329 0019

Barcelona designer chic has converted this old convent opposite the modern-art museum, backed up by Paco Guzman's fusion food.

*Bar Pinotxo, Mercat de la Boqueria, stands 466-470, Rambla St Josep, Barcelona Tel: (93) 317 1731.

It's hard to beat the Catalan earthiness of Pinotxo's tapas and raciónes, with ingredients straight from neighboring market stalls.

*Santa María, Carrer Comerç 17, Barcelona Tel: (93) 315 1227

Paco Guzman packs in those in search of imaginative organic tapas.

Bar Tomas, Carrer Major de Sarria 49, Barcelona Tel: (93) 203 1077

Makes Barcelona's tastiest patatas bravas.

Vascelum, Plaça Santa María 4, Barcelona Tel: (93) 319 0167

Devour your ración of chicken leg with prawns while sitting on the terrace in front of the church of Santa María.

RIOJA AND CASTILE

Restaurante El Candil, Ventura Ruiz Aguilera 14-16, Salamanca Tel: (923) 217239
www.helcom.es/elcandil

A gastronomic monument near the Plaza Mayor tucks in a tiny tapas bar where victuals are washed down by excellent wines.

*José María, Cronista Lecea 11, Segovia Tel: (921) 466017

From suckling pig to complex tapas, this is Castile's foodie Mecca.

*Momo, Calle San Pablo 13-15, Salamanca Tel: (923) 280798

Castile's most stylish tapas bar has ironically taken root in this Renaissance city.

La Mortaraza, Calle José Jauregui 9, Salamanca Tel: (923) 260021

An established venue for meaty regional cuisine, at the bar or in the restaurant. Sample morcilla (blood sausage), oxtail, tongue, or braised partridge.

*Casa Pali, Calle Laurel 11, Logroño Tel: (941) 256795

One of dozens of tapas bars in Logroño's heaving epicenter, and one of the best.

Bar Sebas, Calle Albornoz 3, Logroño Tel: (941) 220196

Stuffed peppers and tortilla de patatas (potato omelette) are the specialties in this popular watering hole of La Laurel.

La Tasquina, Calle Valdelaguila 3, Segovia Tel: (921) 461954

Excellent wines, including cava, head the menu here, joined by choice platters of cheeses, hams, and sausage meats.

MADRID

*Albur, Calle Manuela Malasaña 15, Madrid Tel: (91) 594 2733

Back-to-nature organic products from all over Spain are prepared in post-nueva cocina style in this easygoing tapas bar and restaurant.

Taberna de Antonio Sanchez, Calle Mesón de Paredes 13, Madrid Tel: (91) 539 7826.
The capital's oldest tavern has barely changed since 1830; neither have its snail tapas.

*Bocaito, Calle Libertad 6, Madrid Tel: (91) 532 1219
For a vast choice of Spain's top produce, this is where to go. Try a string of tostadas, gambas (prawns), angulas (baby eel), or smoked crab paté.

Chipén, Calle Cardenal Cisneros 39, Madrid Tel: (91) 445 4385
A Chambéri hot spot for countless classic tapas, from octopus to Burgos blood sausage.

Taberna de Dolores, Plaza de Jesus 4, Madrid Tel: (91) 429 2243
Excellent tapas of top-quality Spanish produce, from seafood to meats and hams.

Los Gatos, Calle Jesus 2, Madrid Tel: (91) 429 3067
Madrid's night cats gravitate here to sample straightforward tapas in an eccentric haven of eclectic 1970s kitsch.

*José Luis, Calle Serrano 89, Madrid Tel: (91) 563 0958
Well established, and with a resident shoe shiner, this is Madrid's foremost tapas and pintxos bar.

Casa Labra, Calle Tetuan 12, Madrid Tel: (91) 531 0081
One hundred and forty years of existence haven't altered the exquisite croquetas.

Lhardy, Carrera de San Jeronimo 8, Madrid Tel: (91) 532 4200
Nineteenth-century elegance reigns in one of Madrid's most reputed restaurants. Caldo is still served at the front as a restorative, backed up by pastry-based snacks.

*Casa Matute, Plaza de Matute 5, Madrid Tel: (91) 429 4384
Obey one of Joaquín Campos's ten tapas commandments and you won't regret it: Andalucía meets Madrid.

THE LEVANTE

Tabernas A Fuego Lento, Calle Caballeros 47, Plaza del Esparto, Valencia Tel: (96) 392 1827
Plates of delicious Iberian produce are served in intimate dining areas in this contemporary tapas restaurant.

*Gambrinus, Plaze de la Reina 19, Valencia

Tel: (96) 392 3191
Beer flows to back up huge portions of tapas with an Anglo-Saxon twist.

*Bodeguilla del Gato, Calle Catalans 10 (Plaza Negrito), Valencia Tel: (96) 391 8235
Hearty tapas and raciónes with a Basque note in Valencia's nocturnal center.

*Mesón de Labradores, Calle Labradores 19, Alicante Tel: (96) 520 4846
The place to go in the back streets of Alicante to sample hearty tapas fare.

*Bodega Montaña, Calle José Benlliure 69, El Cabanyal, Valencia Tel: (96) 367 2314
This combined bar and bodega is a Levante landmark revered by all.

Nou Manolin, Calle Villegas 3, Alicante Tel: (96) 520 0368
Lines form to grab a stool and indulge in delectable, fresh seafood tapas and salads at this upmarket bar.

Meson Pepe Juan, Calle Portalet 1, Calpe Tel: (96) 583 2988
Squid, chicken livers, stuffed eggplant, and tortillas are among the appetizing tapas in this intact survivor of the region's tourist invasion.

Bar Pilár, Moro Zeit 13, Valencia Tel: (96) 391 0497
An early twentieth-century classic for consuming Valencia's renowned clochinas (mussels).

*Santa Companya, Calle Roteros 21, Valencia Tel: (96) 392 2259
Michele Gallana has revived Valencia's longstanding Italian influences in this sharp tapas bar of the Old Quarter.

Bar Serranos, Calle Blanquerias 5, Valencia Tel: (96) 391 7061
A popular, unpretentious tapas bar with a good seafood lineup.

Tasca Angel, Calle Purisima 1, Valencia Tel: (96) 391 7835
There's little room here for anything other than appetizing seafood and snail tapas.

ANDALUCÍA

*Bodegas Campos, Calle Lineros 32, Cordoba Tel: (95) 749 7500 www.bodegascampos.com
Luckily, this labyrinthine restaurant has a tavern at the entrance for lesser mortals to sample tapas portions of its epicurean delights.

*Casablanca, Calle Zaragoza 50, Seville

Tel: (95) 422 4698
Arguably the best of Seville's countless tapas bars, thanks to Manuel Zamora's gastronomic panache.

*Enrique Becerra, Calle Gamazo 2, Seville Tel: (95) 421 3049
One of Seville's most highly rated restaurants also attracts hordes of well-heeled tapas enthusiasts on a daily basis.

*La Eslava, Calle Eslava 5, Seville Tel: (95) 490 6568
Innovative and quality-conscious, La Eslava is one of Seville's best-kept secrets.

*Bar Europa, Calle Siete Revueltas 35 (Plaza del Pan), Seville Tel: (95) 422 1354
Sparkling cava washes down the Catalan-influenced tapas at this elegant bar.

*La Giralda, Calle Mateos Gago 1, Seville Tel: (95) 422 7435
Tiled and vaulted splendor makes a typical Moorish backdrop for a leisurely hour of tapas-consumption.

Habanilla Café, Alameda de Hércules 63, Seville Tel: (95) 490 2718.
Seville's swinging youth pile into this hopping tapas bar on a nightly basis; if you're not young at heart, you may be more comfortable elsewhere.

Casa Morales, Calle Garcia de Vinuesa 11, Seville Tel: (95) 422 1242
Gigantic earthenware jars of olive oil create the backdrop to this traditional tapas bar, which has barely altered since 1850. The tapas are simple but excellent.

Casa Ricardo, Calle Hernan Cortes 2, Seville Tel: (95) 438 9751
Images of the Virgin Mary are plastered over the 100-year-old walls—a divine setting for tapas of bacalao, jamón, meatballs, and succulent croquetas.

Casa Robles, Calle Alvarez Quinteros 58, Seville Tel: (95) 421 3150
A family-owned food institution opposite the cathedral, ensuring a fast flow of quality tapas.

Sol y Sombra, Calle Castilla 149, Triana, Seville Tel: (95) 433 3935
Meaty raciónes are the order of the day in this atmospheric bullfighters' bar that feels like it's straight out of a film set.

GLOSSARY OF TERMS

In collecting these recipes from my favorite tapas chefs in Spain, I selected those with ingredients that were easily available beyond the Iberian frontiers. However, even these sometimes need explaining—as do some tapas terms—so use the following glossary to identify exactly what they are.

aceite de oliva—a blend of refined and virgin olive oils with far less flavor than virgin olive oil. The basic olive oil for frying.

aceite de oliva virgen—virgin olive oil with acidity levels up to four percent, quite mild in flavor.

aceite de oliva virgen extra (primera presión)—extra-virgin olive oil (first cold pressing) with an acidity level below one percent and a distinctive flavor. Ideal for dressings and drizzles.

aioli—similar to mayonnaise, theoretically without the egg yolk, this Catalan sauce is made from garlic, salt, oil, and optional lemon juice. It is, however, hard to make without the yolk.

anchoas—fresh anchovies or salted anchovy fillets in oil.

bacalao—confusingly, the Spanish word refers both to fresh cod and, far more commonly, to salt cod. The latter form is omnipresent throughout the country and comes in numerous qualities, dependent on their origin.

boquerones—anchovies that are pickled in a wine vinegar.

butifarra—mildly peppered Catalan pork sausage, white or black in color, sometimes including breadcrumbs and with a finer texture than *morcilla*.

cecina—cured beef, typical of León in Old Castile, where it is salted, smoked, and cured. Originally made from horse meat, it is served very finely sliced.

chorizo—spicy cooked sausage flavored with paprika, salt, pepper, and garlic. It comes in fresh, smoked, or cured versions. The best is ninety-five percent pork.

embutidos—a generic term for sausage meats, whether cured, cooked, or fresh.

escabeche—pickling brine or marinade, usually made of oil, vinegar, peppercorns, bay leaves, and/or spices.

guindilla—the chili pepper, which is a New World import to Spain, plays a major role in Spanish cooking. Larger ones are generally milder than smaller ones and the hottest are the dried variety. Red chilies (ripened green chilies) have a sweeter flavor.

jamón ibérico—cured ham from Iberian black-coated pigs.

jamón ibérico de bellota—Spain's top cured ham from black-coated pigs fed on acorns in the wild.

jamón serrano—literally "sawn ham": mass-produced and cured, it is similar to prosciutto, and often used in cooked dishes, when it is more thickly sliced.

jamón de York—cured and cooked ham.

morcilla—the Spanish version of blood sausage (made from pig's blood), which may contain pine nuts and/or rice. The best is from Burgos in Old Castile.

Pedro Ximénez—a very sweet sherry often used in cooking.

pil-pil—a garlic and olive oil sauce that is sometimes made green by the addition of parsley (*salsa verde*).

pimientos del piquillo—small red peppers, oozing with sweetness and flavor, often found canned, as they are only grown in Navarra.

pimentón (paprika)—the Spanish have two types: *pimentón de la vera* (from Extremadura), a smoked paprika that comes in hot, sweet, and sweet-sour varieties; and straightforward *pimentón*, sun-dried paprika, also in hot and sweet versions and made in Murcia.

pintxo—canapé-style tapas, originally from the Basque region.

pisto—originally from La Mancha, a more condensed version of ratatouille made from fried peppers, onion, tomato, garlic, zucchini, eggplant.

raciónes—slightly larger portions than tapas.

requesón—a fresh cheese that is similar to ricotta or cottage cheese.

ventresca de atún/bonito—the belly of the tuna fish, regarded as the most tender part and therefore the most sought after. Also found in canned versions at specialty supermarkets.

vinagre—Spaniards use only wine or sherry vinegar, usually red.

Acknowledgments

I would like to thank all the chefs and bar owners featured in this book for responding so positively to my requests, collaborating with such good humor, and feeding our stomachs and souls so magnificently. I am also grateful to the following for their help and advice: Francoçe Butscher at Turmadrid; Tim O'Grady, José Ferri at the Valencia Region Tourist Board; the San Sebastián Convention Bureau; María José Sevilla at the Spanish Embassy, London; Pilár Faro; Mar Mateo; Christopher Branton; Tamsyn Hill; Lorna Scott-Fox, and, not least, our recipe translator Ana Sims, who succeeded in the face of sometimes daunting odds. As the author, I would also like to stress my gratitude to the photographer, Jan Baldwin, who sailed through the shoots with immense serenity and humor, as well as functioning successfully long into the night, and to the designer, Vanessa Courtier, for her endless enthusiasm and creative approach to this book. Thanks also to the star of recipe-testing, Diana Henry, to our spirited gourmet editor, Rebecca Spry, and to the ever-calm Nicky Collings for seeing the project through with such grace.

RECIPE INDEX BY INGREDIENT